D1080400

WATCHERS IN THE SUN

By the same author

WATCHERS BY THE POOL:
The Cats of Mas des Chats

WATCHERS IN THE SUN

LIFE AT MAS DES CHATS

MARGARET REINHOLD

Photographs by William Gooddy

SOUVENIR PRESS

First published 1994 by Souvenir Press Ltd,
43 Great Russell Street, London WC1B 3PA
and simultaneously in Canada

ISBN 0 285 63211 6

Printed in Great Britain by The Bath Press

Typeset by Galleon Typesetting, Ipswich, Suffolk

This account of a period in my life draws on many facets of experience. The
houses in England and France, and the cats who have shared them with me,
are based on fact. The characters I have described are composites of people
I have encountered along the way, not necessarily in the context in which
they appear. No reference is made or intended to any living person.

To William and Nora

My sincere thanks to Françoise van Naeltwijck and Claire McDonald for their great help with the typescript

1

—◇—

Somewhere in the house, in the depths of the night, a cat howled, a wild, fierce cry that sent a shiver of fear into my dreams. The cry was repeated—again and again.

I woke. Through the window, I saw the Provençal moon riding high in the sky, a large moon, striking squares of brilliant light onto the tiled floor.

Again the cry, and this time another cat voice joined in with a loud, wailing protest—two cats quarrelling. The sounds reached a crescendo of anger and distress. I must investigate.

Three a.m. A desolate, lonely hour on a winter's night in Provence. It didn't surprise me to find Monsieur le Gris, largest cat of the household, standing squarely at the top of the stairs confronting a stranger, a stout grey cat I had never seen before.

As defender of the territory le Gris took his duties seriously. In the light of my torch I could see every hair on his body erect, his yellow eyes glaring as he growled and squeaked and howled. Then the beam of the torch caught the intruder's starry eye. He slid quickly and silently down the stairs, melting into the darkness below—and was out through the cat window.

Monsieur le Gris was about to thunder down the stairs in pursuit, but I soothed and restrained him. There was no point in his giving futile chase on this icy night. Through the window I looked down into the moon-dazed garden, stark black and white in the brilliant light. No sign of the strange cat. He'd gone.

All day long the *Mistral* had raged down the valley of the Rhône, roaring in the empty branches of the great trees round the house. With the coming of night the wind had fallen, leaving stillness and silence and frost. This was a night on which all cats of the household preferred, I hoped, to sleep indoors.

They quarrelled for places on the central heating radiators. The craftiest, not always the bravest, were the winners. I counted them by name as I looked for each of them in his or her sleeping place of the moment. They liked to change and swap and shift about the house, as all cats do.

Monsieur le Gris stationed himself, as a rule, in the kitchen where he could survey the cat window. With his great strength and solid body he was a match for any intruding cat, but these visiting cats, often desperately hungry or in need of shelter, sometimes defied him. Le Gris considered himself, uneasily, the leader of the cat community at Mas des Chats. But in his heart he knew that Nero, the proud black cat, was in reality top cat. Sometimes Monsieur le Gris jostled and tried to hustle Nero, but Nero responded with calm and dignified disdain. Nero was growing old now and he no longer involved himself in brawls with strangers. He preferred to stand aside as a spectator. This night he had hardly stirred from his sleep on a mat near the dining-room door.

Baby was in the kitchen. She had become hopelessly and obsessively attached to Monsieur le Gris, followed him everywhere and slept, if possible, within inches of where he lay.

Jaunty Oedipus, the only uncastrated cat, was asleep in an exhausted tangle of long grey limbs on a chair under the dining-room table. Out all day and half the night on some wild excursion, he had returned, starving and exhausted, shortly before I went to sleep.

His gentle mother, Hélène, was upstairs on a bedroom radiator.

In another room was glorious Katy, irrepressible vagabond and ragamuffin. The last was Lily, the English cat who had come with me from Hampshire years before. Ineffably beautiful still, with her radiant white coat and topaz eyes, she had retired from the hustle and bustle of life at the *mas*. She lived upstairs, a quiet dowager, keeping herself to herself, happy with her little trays of food, her litter box, the bunches of young grass I picked for her to nibble, her memories.

Baby, Katy, Hélène, Oedipus, Monsieur le Gris, Nero and Lily. I counted them, like counting beads on a string, and looked to the stars, pale in the light of the moon, to watch over them.

I went back to my room, followed by Monsieur le Gris, tail upright, a smug expression on his fine face, a cat who felt he had fought for his country like a brave soldier and deserved a reward. I gave him some cat biscuits which he ate with satisfaction. He jumped on my bed, carefully avoiding Caramel, the little dog already established on one corner. Caramel could snap when pushed too far. They settled down and I fell asleep again.

8

Monsieur le Gris considered himself, uneasily, the leader of the cat community at Mas des Chats, but in reality he knew that Nero was top cat.

2

———◇———

My house in Provence was an old stone farmhouse—a *mas*—hidden among abandoned fields and rows of cypress trees, not far from a small town where Romans and pre-Romans used to live, Saint-Rémy-de-Provence.

I'd made up my mind to settle in France, in the south and the sun, when, seven years earlier, I had given up my medical practice in London. At first I had imagined I'd find a house like those I remembered from my childhood at the Cape of Good Hope—a house which stood alone on the edge of the sea, bleached by the sun, cooled by winds coming across oceans, where the air smelled of salt and of the warm vegetation growing on the rim of a beach of soft white sand. But once I had started to look, I knew I must change my ideas.

I searched in various areas along the Mediterranean coast-line, or a few miles inland from the sea.

First, I inspected the Côte d'Azur, where the climate allows mimosa to flower in the gardens in the spring. The house agent, a small, quiet man, drove me around from house to house. The properties he showed me were all terrible—impossible to imagine living in them—perhaps because I could only afford a comparatively modest price. The house agent didn't encourage me to choose one of them. Uncomplaining, he showed me others.

In the evening, as I left him, I said, 'Tomorrow, then, I'll look at the rest on your list.'

'Not tomorrow,' he said. 'I don't leave the office tomorrow.' Glancing at my surprised face he said, 'Tomorrow I am fasting.'

I was taken aback.

'I hope you're not ill. I'm sorry to have made you drive around if you're not well . . .'

'No, no! I'm quite well. I fast for one day every week.' And he added, as I said nothing, in an undertone hard to catch, 'I do it to remember all the people in the world who are starving.'

I have never forgotten his day of hunger, pondered on it, felt sympathy and liking for that quiet man. The Côte d'Azur houses, I suppose, some of the wealthiest people in the world. Perhaps his fast was a way of coping with guilt—or his clients' lack of guilt.

The day after his fast we drove around again, to see more impossible houses. The car crawled in heavy traffic up and down the narrow roads. It was early spring, quite out of the holiday season.

He said, during one prolonged hold-up, 'You realise you can't possibly stay here in July and August. During those months you must go away. It's unbearable here.'

I'm sure what he said was true.

Next day, I left to look for a house elsewhere, although mimosa flowered in every garden.

I looked then in the eastern Pyrenees, not far from the sea. There, the snow fields of Mount Canigou fill the sky. Green foothills and great heights fall away suddenly, to a shimmering plain which stretches to the shore.

The young house agent told me he had been born and grown up in a little town, Amilie-les-Bains, which lies under Canigou. He had gone away to live in Africa for a while, but his longing for the mountains brought him back. The day he returned and saw Mount Canigou again, he wept with joy.

I stayed in Amilie-les-Bains, a pleasant thermal station, in a charming hotel where almost every guest, taking the cure, brought a dog into the dining-room at meal-times. There was a plaque on the mountain-side nearby, put there by the citizens in honour of their beloved Mayor, murdered by the *barbares Nazis*.

I could understand the house agent's feelings. The beauty of those mountains and valleys sinks deep into a person's being. But I found the houses and villages too remote, the roads winding and narrow and liable to be blocked by snow in winter.

I would try elsewhere.

That autumn, in England, I saw an advertisement for houses in Provence, placed in the newspaper by a house agent in Saint-Rémy-de-Provence.

I replied, was tempted to investigate and there I found my *mas*.

'Here in Provence we say "*mas*",' said the house agent, pronouncing the 's'. 'The people from Paris say "*mah*"!' He must have liked the sound he made with '*mah*' because he repeated the word a few times, musingly.

———————◇———————

My decision to leave England was a hard one to make. I had a house in the Hampshire downs at Ashford, a much loved house, among cornfields and beechwoods. It was isolated, a little remote. At night, the animals of the woods visited the garden—foxes and badgers, crossing and recrossing in their search for food—and by day the garden was full of birds.

Two very English cats, Rosie and Lily, shared that house with me—and loved it too, I know. There had also been a third cat, Mews, found abandoned and ill in the streets of London. Rescued and cared for, that beautiful ginger tom was taken down to live in the Hampshire house. Rosie and Lily were adopted as kittens to be his companions.

Mews was the love of Lily's life. He became ill and died, to her and my great sorrow, shortly before the move to France.

When I made that move, I took Rosie and Lily with me. For me, France was to be a new beginning, a door opening to fresh woods . . . For the cats, I hoped they would adapt to a strange country and a different climate—and eventually they did.

The house in Provence had great beauty, a beauty that was harsher and stronger than that of the gentle house in England. All around it was a countryside that never failed to excite the senses. Not far away, to the south, there rose the strange and moving shapes of the rocky Alpilles, blue, pine-covered hills that are the last outpost of the Alps. Between the farmhouse and the hills there were farms, each with its fields protected from the *Mistral* by great hedges of cypresses and rows of tall poplars. And there were groves of olive trees and orchards of peach and apricot and a canal that fed the streams which surrounded every field—and surrounded also the small shady garden of my farmhouse and its vineyard.

To begin with, Rosie, Lily and I were uneasy exiles. Slowly we settled down. Rosie and Lily became familiar with their territory. They understood the boundaries of the garden with its great trees and old

All around the house was a countryside that never failed to excite the senses.

walls where lizards could be hunted in the sun. They were fascinated by the green swimming pool. They enjoyed strolling in the vineyard. Rosie, more daring than Lily, explored the neighbouring fields for mice.

After a while I came to love the house in Provence as I'd loved the house in England.

The seven years went swiftly by. They were light and brilliant years, charged with the special intensity that life has in Provence—translucent years, leaving memories of England unclouded and vivid in my mind.

And they were years during which Rosie and Lily and I were joined by a number of French cats, Provençal cats, some of whom eventually made their home with us.

The French cats turned up one by one, coming upon the farmhouse in their search for food and shelter. They were abandoned or lost, or ill-treated and hungry.

Realising that there were starving animals in the hills and fields around the house, I put out a big bowl of food by the stream at night. The hungry cats would come to eat, and a few, who came night after night, began to be seen, shy but brave, during the day as well as in the dark. After a time some of them ventured inside the house.

So arrived Hélène, the young elegant white and black creature, who gave birth to two kittens on the hillside just above the *mas*. We called the kittens Oedipus and Emilie—Oedipus, because he seemed to be so attached to his mother well into his adult life. Hélène brought her two kittens down to the *mas* when she considered they were old enough, and established herself in a spare room which opened on to the terrace.

There was Maman, a sweet-natured, rather elderly cat who arrived in midwinter with her very young kitten whom we called Baby. The two were inseparable, a discreet and charming couple.

There was also Nero, the great black noble animal who became head of the household cats.

And there was Monsieur le Gris, the grey and white cat of massive physique but insecure emotions. He had a severe inferiority complex which made him anxious and jealous, always afraid one of the other cats was getting better treatment and more love than he was. But he had intelligence and courage and some very endearing characteristics. I was always either angry with him for his tantrums and bullying of the younger cats, or full of warmth and affection for him with his babyish behaviour.

One of his *bêtes noires* was Katy—literally black, with a white waistcoat and ruff—a small energetic urchin, rescued as a kitten by friends from the streets of Saint-Rémy and given to me when they had to return to England.

And most loved of all was Bruno, a half-Siamese kitten who turned up with an all-white companion called Blanco, as refugees from a

Eventually all the feline members of the household lived more or less amicably together.

family who lived nearby. They had been thrown out because it was feared they might sit on the face of a newly born child and suffocate her.

It took some time for these cats to be accepted by Rosie and Lily—and by one another—but eventually all the feline members of the household lived more or less amicably together.

I named the farmhouse 'Mas des Chats'.

There was also a small dog. Her name was Caramel. She too was a refugee from a nearby farmhouse where she had been neglected and ill-treated. Caramel had decided to escape to Mas des Chats and she refused to return to her original home, a state of affairs accepted by all. Cats and dog accepted one another peacefully and the animals formed, for while, a close community.

But the cat population at Mas des Chats was never static. There were always comings and goings.

After five years, there were some deaths and departures.

My beloved Rosie became ill and died, as did the young, beautiful and enchanting cat Bruno, whose death I found devastating. His companion Blanco went off one cold winter's night and never returned. Another loss was dear Maman, who became increasingly feeble and ill before she died.

New cats arrived.

Some stayed. Some disappeared again.

The older cats grew old, became invalids in time.

Young cats strayed in.

And there was also a kitten.

3

The window of the kitchen at Mas des Chats was always open. Through it day and night, at all seasons, the cats of the household came and went as they pleased. Other cats also came, discovering the place perhaps from the smell of food or by watching the household cats at their exits and entrances.

The window looked to the south. Pieces of flat metal fringed with large, curved spikes, hand-forged by a local blacksmith and sealed into the stone windowsill, prevented burglars and large dogs from entering. But cats could negotiate their way with ease—as could the little dog Caramel. Sunlight and moonlight poured into the house through this window, and outside a lamp was installed on the wall of the house and was lit at night, so making the terrace dramatically beautiful, with its olive trees and flowers illuminated.

I placed a white garden table under the window with a chair beside it and beneath the chair a flat log of wood. Cats—and Caramel—could then enter and leave by leaping up and down a series of steps. They were also able to look into the garden or the house before making their final leap, so avoiding dangerous dogs, or what might have been, in their view, dangerous humans.

At night there was food for hungry cats of the neighbourhood, placed in bowls beneath the window. I had had to stop putting the dishes of food in the garden by the stream when a gang of starving dogs began to roam about the countryside, desperately searching for food. They would eat anything and everything they could find. The cat food disappeared in a moment. Sometimes even the bowls would be snatched and left in the fields nearby.

Because the dogs seemed famished I put out food for them also— large dishes of bread and milk and dog biscuits. In the morning the dishes had been polished smooth by hungry tongues.

One night, I was sitting in the kitchen writing when I felt myself observed. A huge Alsatian had put his face in at the cat window and was staring at me. He ran off as I stood up.

During the winter, the window was largely covered by a transparent plastic screen which the gardener, Monsieur Mercier, had cleverly constructed. Two small squares were left open for the cats and Caramel. She would rush out—more noisily and clumsily than the cats, but just as easily—and bark hysterically at the visiting dogs, whatever their size. This gave her great pleasure. The dogs seemed afraid of her and made off, temporarily only. They sneaked back after a while to finish the food. The cats of the household liked to gather after they had been fed themselves to watch the comings and goings of the 'outside cats'.

In the old days at Ashford in Hampshire, the English cats, Lily and Rosie and Mews, used to sit together on the edge of the lawn to watch the foxes who came to eat. The foxes slid stealthily in from the fields and woods under a great beech hedge. There, too, I put out bread and

The window in the kitchen was always open to allow the cats to come and go as they pleased. Le Gris would sit there on guard, blocking it with his large bulk.

milk and scraps for them. Often there would be several foxes and sometimes cubs squealing and jostling for the food.

For the cats, this nightly event seemed very entertaining, like going to the theatre. The spectacle of the arrival and departure of the 'outside cats' was equally interesting for many of those at Mas des Chats—Baby, le Gris, Nero, Hélène, and sometimes Katy.

Monsieur le Gris often became impatient and resentful of the strange cats eating what he considered to be his food in his kitchen. He would start complaining, making threatening cries, or he would try to eat the food himself or cover the dishes with hypothetical earth, scratching the tiled floor with his strong paw.

Baby, following his example, made small meowing noises to show her disapproval.

Sometimes le Gris would simply try to block the entrance of the window by lying on the radiator just beneath it, his large bulk making it dangerous, even impossible, for them to get through. Here he would be joined by the adoring Baby, the two lying serenely nose to tail.

When the warm weather came, the plastic shield was taken down from the window—a happy moment which meant that summer had truly arrived.

I wondered how the cats looked on this window. For the outside cats it meant a dangerous running of the gauntlet, yet a passage to vital food supplies. For the cats of the household it was the barrier between the fascinating wild world of the garden and vineyard and the comfortable but dull domesticity of the house.

For me, the window had a symbolic, mythical meaning—the gate of an old walled city, the portcullis of a medieval fortress. Within the house I felt my cats were safe. Beyond the window it seemed, at night, there was infinite danger for them. When darkness came I longed to have them in their places indoors. Left to me, once all were in, I would have shut the window. But this I couldn't do. Anxious as it made me, I must let them lead their lives in freedom. Wild or half-wild, they couldn't bear to be imprisoned—and this I understood.

4

—◇—

My neighbours at Mas des Chats were farmers, *paysans*. On the eastern border of the *mas* was a large old farmhouse divided into three parts. In the middle lived Monsieur and Madame Corbet who also owned several of the fields around the farmhouse, and fields towards the road—the old road to Arles—and beyond it. They grew vegetables, as now all the farmers did, although years ago it used to be flowers that the *paysans* grew for the seed; the whole countryside around Saint-Rémy-de-Provence was under flowers. Now only a few people in the neighbourhood grew flowers. There were one or two fields near Mas des Chats covered in velvety petunias, crimson and purple, or portulaca, a carpet of jewels, brilliant red and yellow and white and pink, sparkling in the sun.

The Corbets were infinitely kind to me and became good friends.

On the western border was an eccentric man and his gentle wife. The two worked harder in their fields than any people I've ever seen. Not only did they grow a huge variety of fruit and vegetables which they sold with great success, but they also cultivated their garden and their large row of potted geraniums. The geraniums could have won prizes for size and intensity of colour. In the garden, they pruned forsythias into the shapes of giant baskets. Monsieur Moret, the farmer, was, I think, a difficult and shy man. He had quarrelled vigorously with his father to whom he wouldn't speak, Madame Corbet told me, and this embittered him. I knew him only slightly but had no problems with him.

To the north of Mas des Chats, that is, behind it, was a large farm populated by a large family, the Mabeilles.

There were several brothers and sisters. Some, not all, lived on the farm in various houses and some of their children lived there too. They were a disturbed lot, the most seriously mentally ill being Giselle, who lived with her mother in a dilapidated row of buildings. Her mother, it was said, was too fond of Pastis.

Giselle used to visit me from time to time. We communicated somehow and she seemed to find comfort in these visits. She had quarrelled with most of the other members of the family—and with my other neighbours.

In general she was very much disliked. 'Never let her in,' Monsieur Corbet advised me, 'you'll never get rid of her.' But I did manage to persuade her to go. After a brief conversation I would say, 'I'm so sorry but I must go now,' and smile and hold out my hand which she would take, smile also, bow and say, '*Au revoir*, Margaretta,' and she would leave. She kept a number of cats, whom she loved. Many of our conversations were about cats. Hers came frequently to eat at Mas des Chats; I think she hardly fed them.

'What do you give them to eat?' I would ask. She would pause to consider.

Then, '*Croquettes*!' she said, and then something incomprehensible and then, '*et des boites*'—but this, I think, was fantasy. She could never have had enough tins to feed her many cats—or, in fact, enough *croquettes*.

Her cats were often ill, died or disappeared. The females had kittens which were drowned—by whom I didn't ask. If a cat died she would telephone me to tell me. On the telephone she was completely incomprehensible. She shouted, and the line was always bad, crackling and faint. I could often only hear my name as pronounced by her, Margaretta, and one or two key words. Giselle hardly noticed my irrelevant replies and continued a bouncing monologue until I interrupted and said, '*Au revoir.*'

5

—◇—

Rain fell, strong, vertical rain—solid water which had been sucked up into the sky from the sea in the south—Mediterranean rain moving across the land in a series of unrelenting showers. Rain splashed and gurgled and slid heavily from the roof to bounce in great fountains on the stones of the terrace below, then to seep into the *mas* under the glass-paned doors.

The household cats lay bored and restive here and there about the house.

Suddenly, without warning, a young cat, drenched, leapt through the cat window into the kitchen, ballet-dancer light, butterfly brown, dappled, mottled, unconcerned. She was closely followed by Maurice, fierce one-eyed cat of my Moroccan neighbours, the former owners of Caramel, who launched himself upon her as if to mate. But she shrugged him off, dancing away to a far corner of the room, he following adamantly.

Sugar, Brown Sugar, a rare and beautiful tortoiseshell, had arrived at Mas des Chats.

Not that I thought, at that moment, that she was going to stay. She looked like someone's most loved cat, temporarily strayed from home. Cheerfully she flitted about the kitchen, eluding, escaping Maurice, whom I sent away at the next lull in the rain. And she, giving a deep contralto hum, settled down happily to a dish of food I put before her. Sugar wasn't used to hunger; her little body was rounded and well padded.

It was quite clear that nobody had ever hurt Sugar. She wasn't afraid of people or dogs or other cats. Serenely certain of her attractiveness, she expected to be accepted and cherished.

After her meal, she enjoyed having her coat dried with a towel and she climbed firmly onto my lap.

Then she began to sneeze.

She must have caught a cold in the rain.

Her sneezes were a long series of quick, staccato explosions—one after another like rapid gunfire.

Brown Sugar, a rare and beautiful tortoiseshell, had arrived at Mas des Chats.

She coughed a little.

Nevertheless, her coat shone, earth-coloured, wine-coloured, with paler patches like sunlight on fallen leaves.

Where could she have come from? How had she found her way to the cat window in the downpour? Had Maurice chased her from her home, mistakenly believing she was on heat? Was she—an alarming idea—pregnant?

Without much hope—I had tried so often before with animals who seemed lost—I did a tour of the neighbouring houses to enquire everywhere whether anyone had lost a young tortoiseshell cat.

No one had. At *mas* after *mas* I received the same answer, the same shaking of the head, the same: No, next door, they only had dogs. No, they had never seen a tortoiseshell cat in the neighbourhood.

I returned discouraged. Sugar was an exceptionally tame and confident cat. She had certainly belonged to a caring owner. What was more, her claws had been cut to prevent her doing damage when scratching—to a child? To furniture?

But it was equally clear that Sugar was about to become the eighth cat at Mas des Chats.

For some time I hoped that Sugar, the rain over, would find her own way home. I tried to get her to accompany me on little walks, now in one direction, now in another.

But Sugar wasn't really interested in little walks. She showed not the slightest inclination to leave, not the slightest anxiety about staying at the *mas*. She felt quite comfortable, thank you very much, and enjoyed the company of the other cats with whom, in general, she got on well. She liked me, she thought. On the whole, the food was good, the accommodation reasonable. She loved the garden and could see at once it was good mousing territory.

And she very much hoped that with careful medical attention she would be able to get rid of her cold.

Her cold, however, continued. It was possible to tell exactly where Sugar was in the garden by the staccato explosions of sneezing. She didn't seem particularly disturbed by the cold, except that at certain times it became worse. She had courses of antibiotics. Sometimes she was better, but there were times when she was seriously ill with

Sugar was exceptionally tame and confident, and a passionate hunter.

complications in the form of pneumonia with a high fever. The vet warned me she might die if the antibiotics failed to cure the infections. Throughout her illness, Sugar remained serene. She was polite to the vet, affectionate to me.

She survived. We discovered that sulphonamides helped her. She grew stronger and bigger and, although at first her cold returned whenever the weather was bad, gradually the sound of her sneezes died out. Sugar seemed to have been cured.

A gentle animal, sensitive and nervous when attacked, she was at the mercy of Katy who loved to terrify her. Katy leapt out at her from behind bushes and terrace pots. Sugar screamed and lay on her back. Katy towered over her, a small but dangerous enemy. Sometimes I had to rescue Sugar, who was hurt and upset that anyone should want to be unpleasant to her.

Her other adversary was Monsieur le Gris, who liked to bully the younger cats. But Sugar could hardly believe that he would seriously wish to do her harm. She took the wind out of his sails by not noticing his threatening gestures. To save his pride, he pretended he was really just cleaning his whiskers and wasn't interested in her. But every now and then he succeeded in upsetting her. She was baffled and offended.

'What's wrong with him?' she seemed to ask. It would never have occurred to Sugar to say to herself, 'What's wrong with me to make him behave like that to me?'

Sugar knew very well there was absolutely nothing wrong with her. Her unusual face, with its many colours and large amber eyes, looked wild. Her dappled coat had the texture of velvet. She was a passionate hunter. Lizards, dragonflies, moths, little mice in the field were captured and often slain unless I could rescue them. She darted and dashed and flew in the air. Sometimes she was too busy to eat and had to rush off in the middle of a meal. Her voice was a deep contralto, used to greet everyone—people, cats and dogs. Cheerful, good-natured, purring Sugar—she was a lovable cat and I loved her.

6

Nero had come upon the Mas des Chats, like many other cats and dogs, when ranging round in his search for food. He was a keen traveller, as I was to discover later, and he went far from home.

When he found that food was available at Mas des Chats, he became a regular visitor. He was bony and thin, his coat dull and rough, and he was full of worms.

He belonged to two men, tenants of Roger Mabeille, my farmer neighbour.

One day these men went off to live in the town, leaving Nero behind, and once it became clear to him that he had been abandoned, he installed himself at Mas des Chats. But each day he went back to the house his owners had rented, a haphazard attachment to the main big farmhouse of the Mabeille farm.

He took a path which crossed the stream on the northern border of Mas des Chats. Then he trotted on, going steadily northwards, through a copse of scrub oak and down the stony hill to a bridge crossing a wider stream, arising from a spring. He then arrived at a collection of sheds and farm buildings where he was well known to the various farm workers. His previous owners' house was at the end of a row of apartments converted from the huge old main house.

On his way there he had to pass Mademoiselle Mabeille—a stout Ophelia—and her mother who sat bemused on a rickety chair in the shade of a great lime tree, sipping from her glass of Pastis.

Mademoiselle Mabeille, Giselle, took a great interest in him and knew him by the name he'd been given by his previous owners: Vivaldi. When she called on me from time to time she always asked after him. She claimed that he was the father of one of her cats, a black one who, she said, had the same little patch of white hair on his belly as Nero-Vivaldi had.

Nero was familiar to the various members of the Mabeille family on account of his wanderings all over the farm. He used to hunt, depending partly on mice or birds or anything he could find for his food. Then he would lie in the sun or the shade, resting under the scrub oaks, or in

He would lie in the sun, resting under the scrub oaks.

one of the packing sheds where the lettuces and carrots were put in boxes and sacks for the market at Saint-Etienne-du-Grès.

When he became a cat of the household, I took it for granted that he would make long journeys and excursions—and he did. But I didn't bargain for the fact that he might be away for two, three or four days at a time, so giving me anxiety about his safety. Once he spent ten days away from home. I had given up hope when he came bounding in through the cat window as if he had just woken up from a ten-minute nap.

When I criticised him he stared at me innocently with his golden eyes. 'Who? Me? But what have I done?'

I couldn't explain—a couple of sleepless nights, several long tramps and car rides round the neighbourhood, asking and asking in vain . . . 'You have exhausted me,' I told his uncomprehending, bland, black face, 'please don't do it again!' He purred loudly and rubbed his soft body against my legs.

7

—◇—

Baby was accustomed to having deep relationships. Her first great love had been her mother with whom she had arrived at Mas des Chats as a kitten. Baby and Maman had been inseparable for years. They had lain together in the house and garden, taken their walks together, hunted together, played together, washed their coats together and slept in the same basket.

But while Maman was a tame, gentle cat, used to being handled by human beings, Baby was wild—afraid of people being close to her, untouchable, like any feral cat. She would come near enough to eat in the kitchen with the other cats, but it was impossible to pick her up. Her intense relationship with her mother had ended only a few weeks before Maman's death, when Maman was absolutely exhausted and ill. Baby then quietly withdrew, although she still gave Maman a good wash from time to time, which her mother seemed to find comforting. During Maman's last illness, Baby had developed a passion for Bruno, the beautiful half-Siamese cat who died of cat leukaemia. Bruno, during his short life, was kind to Baby, affectionate sometimes, but his real love was the English cat Rosie. Baby looked up to Rosie and admired her, but Rosie also died, not long after Bruno's death. And some weeks later, Maman too was dead.

When Bruno died Baby had been distraught and took some time to recover. After Maman's death she didn't seem very disturbed but she must have missed her mother greatly. For a while she remained alone and lonely. Then she began to look around for a mother substitute. To my and the cats' astonishment, she chose Monsieur le Gris. He was notorious for his bad manners, his rough bullying, ungracious ways and, on a bad day, unrestrained temper tantrums. But Baby had made up her mind. She seemed to have decided that not only would she make a good friend out of him, she would manage to persuade him to love her. Valiant little Baby went through many hard times with le Gris and there were many setbacks, but she was undeterred. In the end, she succeeded, and Monsieur le Gris accepted her as a close companion. More than that, there was considerable physical rapport. She and he

To my and the cats' astonishment, Baby chose Monsieur le Gris as a mother substitute. Where he went, she was always close by.

were so closely linked that we began to call them Monsieur and Madame le Gris. Where he went, she went. Where he lay down, she would lie—as near to him as possible. When he jumped in through the cat window, Baby was always close behind. If the door was open, they would come into the kitchen in tandem, an ill-assorted but charming couple—rough yeoman le Gris, a giant cat, and pretty Baby, round and feminine, a quarter his size. While they were waiting to be given their plates of food, Baby would lie down beside Monsieur le Gris and push her little head under his chin. She would meow like a kitten. Le Gris then began to lick and nibble her head and the back of her neck and sometimes he washed her from head to tail. Baby shut her eyes in bliss. When he stopped licking, Baby would meow again and push her head forward. Quite often le Gris went on nibbling and caressing her, but sometimes, getting bored, he began to growl and snap. Baby would become nervous and withdraw. Her attitude was that she knew her le Gris was a difficult man, but a good one at heart. Give him time, be patient, he'll settle down again. He's probably hungry—it's understandable, isn't it?

And she would wait quietly for the right moment to approach him again.

There were times when Monsieur le Gris was in a very bad mood.

Then he could be so indifferent and so hostile to Baby that humans observing them felt sorry for her. An Englishwoman who lived with her husband in the little house in the garden from time to time, found le Gris' rejection of Baby almost unbearable.

'Like all those women who choose the wrong man—like life . . .' said Karen. She grimaced slightly, suffering pain for Baby, her own pain, presumably from her own experiences of life.

When le Gris was at his most unpleasant, Baby withdrew into herself and went off alone into the fields. I would see her small black and white figure trudging up the gravel road past the vines, making for some sheltered spot where she liked to lie.

She would return a few hours later, stoical and self-contained. If she met le Gris somewhere on her way home he was likely to be in a better mood, so they would come together, side by side. Then Baby would recover some cheerfulness and confidence.

Le Gris did, I think, eventually become genuinely attached to Baby. He seemed to miss her when she wasn't around and he would pay special attention to his grooming of her. Sometimes he would try to sit on her. She disappeared completely under his fluffy white belly, but that didn't seem to upset her. She emerged undamaged and happy, urging him to nibble her ears just once more.

The other cats and I watched their performance in amazement, wondering, I'm sure, what on earth Baby saw in le Gris (he was not a popular figure in the kitchen). Hélène, who was the only one of them with maternal feelings but who took a cynical view of life, might, I think, have commented on the fact that le Gris was at least twice Baby's age and four times as stout—and she might have added that, of course, Baby had never known her father and was probably searching for a father substitute. My own view was that Baby was trying to make a mother out of le Gris and being quite successful at it. Whatever was behind it, she was obsessively fixed on him. Whenever possible she was close to him.

The attachment had its disadvantages. One autumn, the coldest and rainiest ever, Baby became ill. She began to sneeze and cough and developed blisters on her nose—a severe virus infection. I'm sure she felt wretched, but nothing would stop her following le Gris. Out into

When he was at his most unpleasant, she withdrew into herself and went off alone.

the rain they went, in through the cat window and out again as the will took le Gris. I tried protecting her with an injection of slow-release antibiotic (I had become adept at giving cats a quick injection while they had their heads in their plates of food), but this helped only partially. She became more ill, coughing and sneezing vigorously. I couldn't catch her to keep her indoors and helplessly watched her trot out with le Gris, day and night, into the icy winds and the rain.

But one afternoon I found her on a settee in the dining-room, a collapsed little heap of misery, hardly able to struggle when I put her in a basket to take her to the vet.

Docteur Lamartin, kind and helpful as always, found she had a soaring temperature and prescribed a course of another antibiotic. Baby lay limply on the examination table and was in no condition to protest.

At last there was an opportunity to keep her indoors. I shut her in the salon by herself.

Poor Baby looked like a trapped wild creature. She was terrified— and longed to be with le Gris.

But in her weakened state I was able to cuddle and caress her and this she seemed to enjoy. Gradually she relaxed. When she was able to eat, I brought her little dishes of her favourite foods and cat biscuits. I visited her often, talking to her, touching her, soothing her, caressing her again and again, gently.

And then some very mysterious, inexplicable, magical transference of trust and affection occurred between Baby and me.

Quite suddenly, she was no longer afraid of me.

She began to enjoy being shut in the salon, in warmth and comfort. She enjoyed my visits, squeaking and meowing at me as she squeaked at le Gris, jumping up on the sofa next to where I sat, rolling on her back with her paws in the air in pleased anticipation of a massage of her tummy, purring hard. The time came when her fever had left her. She was almost well again. The door of the salon was opened and she could have escaped to freedom. But Baby was happy to remain. She had made a number of little resting places for herself. Perched on the edge of the small piano, tucked into the cushions on a chair, curled up on a stool beside a radiator, she now thought of the salon as hers, her safe territory.

When I visited her she ran to greet me, uttering her unfamiliar little cries, falling once more on her back so that the white whiteness of the fur of her underside was exposed again. She purred with a squeaky purr.

She had a round black spot under her chin and each white paw was barred on the underside with black. She stared at me, unafraid, with her brilliant green eyes. She had the extreme innocence of a small furry wild creature, and the charm of a big soft toy. I felt I had never really known Baby until this time, so much of her character had been hidden in her wildness.

She still sought out le Gris and still enticed him to love her. But now she had an alternative—or an additional—source of affection. The effect on her general spirits was remarkable. She became frisky, light-hearted and gay.

Now there was a little glitter to Baby, a *joie de vivre* which I hoped would endure.

8

—◇—

I grew to know all the cats who came into the house through the cat window—at least those who appeared before midnight. The numbers varied from time to time and the groups changed, but, for a while, there would be a stable gathering of visitors.

Every now and then a cat disappeared and was never seen again.

The cats of the neighbourhood—and that included my own—were permanently at risk. They each had, perhaps, nine lives, but they quickly ran through these, it seemed. Cats have a repertoire of tricks which help them to escape danger—quick leaps, sudden sideways contortions and spurts up a tree—but they are happy-go-lucky adventurers, recklessly obstinate and lethally inquisitive.

Mine, I felt, balanced on the edge of a chasm doing somersaults and dances. I could do nothing but watch helplessly. And I had to watch, also, the instinctive drives which obliterate reason and judgement. Oedipus went off in rain and storm and bitter cold—and stayed away—to find a mate. Monsieur le Gris, after bullying and tormenting all those members of the household he considered intruders—which meant everyone except sycophantic Baby—sturdily faced savage un-castrated males at the cat window, who were ready to tear him to pieces if he prevented them from reaching their dinners. Procreation and protection of territory, these were of paramount importance. The species had to be preserved, not the individual.

And, in fact, if one of the outside cats vanished, a replacement quite quickly turned up.

For some time there had been, among others, two tabbies, one with a white chest. The plain one had a slight squint, made little meowing cries, two at a time, to indicate hunger and ate enormous meals. The white-chested cat was fiercer and silent but also ate a huge amount each night. They were big strong males, the two of them, and rivals who quarrelled often.

There was also a charming black cat with a round face, tame and talkative and very good-natured, who would demand food in a shrill, agitated little voice if none was available. This cat resembled Nero, although he was slimmer and smaller. There were two cats belonging to Giselle Mabeille, comical-looking, black and white, both with a white blaze down the very centre of their black faces. They must have been related to one another.

There was a fine, square, quiet black and white cat who came from a long way away. I saw him from time to time making his way down the little road leading from the old road to Arles.

And there was a sad, worried old cat with very short legs like a feline dachshund, who had been coming for food to Mas des Chats for years. His coat was a confused muddle of black and white.

The outside cats ate voraciously, unlike the cats of the household. They swallowed their food in great snatches, hurriedly. The inside cats took delicate fragments from their dishes, one crumb at a time.

The outside cats turned up stealthily after dark, never in daylight. They hurried away, once satisfied, to mysterious destinations. Some may have had good homes, but the majority were down-and-outs.

The household cats reacted to these cats each according to his or her character. They positioned themselves comfortably in the kitchen, watched and waited. Sometimes one or another would make a comment, or would squeak or growl or grumble.

The outside cats recognised that they were on foreign territory and were, on the whole, nervous, discreet and nimble. They hid under chairs when they sensed hostility and they replied perfunctorily to challenging remarks on the part of the household cats. Sometimes they fought with one another, howling and miauling, rather to the amusement of the 'inside' cats.

One morning in the garden, Monsieur Mercier called to me in a voice of alarm and emergency.

'*Madame, Madame, venez vite. Votre chat noir est mort!*'

'*Mais ce n'est pas possible! Je viens de le voir.* I saw him only a moment ago!'

I rushed to where Monsieur Mercier stood by a row of small bushes which surrounded a rose bed.

There, under one of the bushes, was the body of a black cat, cold and stiff.

To my relief it was not Nero, but the 'outside cat' whom I knew so

Monsieur Mercier at work in the garden. One day he called to me that he had found a dead cat under a rose bush. He thought it was Nero.

well, and that was bad enough. He must have crept under the bush to die, ill, injured, poisoned . . . impossible to tell.

This happening intensified my fear for my cats. Whatever had caused the death of the black cat could equally well destroy a member of the household.

I asked Monsieur Mercier to bury him. Whoever had owned him— he was so tame and affectionate he must have had a home—would perhaps be anxious, searching for him, waiting for him to return. When next Giselle Mabeille called I asked her, casually, did she by any chance have a black cat?

She shook her head, with the blank, distant expression she had when her mind was journeying far from the immediate situation. She was listening to inner voices and was not concerned with black or any other cats.

Someone else was sorrowing over his disappearance or hoping against hope that he would return.

My French improved as time went on, became more fluent, less formal. I learnt new words, using my dictionary as I read the newspapers. After a while, I realised that many of the new words were to do with wars and violence and human misery. My increased vocabulary reflected the times in which I lived—although perhaps all times in the history of men and women have always been the same.

Blindé, I learned, meant armoured car and *char* a tank. *Abattre* was to shoot down, *ravisseurs* were kidnappers, *mitraillé* meant machine-gunned, *obus* a shell and *famine* starvation.

And night after night the images chased across the television screen—flies buzzing round the bodies of Africans dying of starvation; bloody corpses carried out of bombed hospitals; tiny orphans of war being transported to safety in buses; people trampling one another underfoot in a desperate scramble to reach the hand-out of half a loaf of bread; despairing old women struggling along snow-covered roads with small bundles of their most precious possessions, escaping, if they could, from gunfire; blood on pavements, blood on walls.

From the human disasters, I turned to the cats, transferring to them the anxiety of a world out of control.

I became passionate about their safety, driven to supervise the movements of this motley crew of little animals who represented the small and vulnerable, but—being cats—they refused to be supervised. There was no way I could ensure their survival.

9

---◇---

Provence was a master of the unexpected, the surprise. There was, as a background to the sometimes astonishing events, the drama of the landscape with the ever-changing light, the evolving sunsets. There was also the explosive growth of plants and trees and vegetation in general—as well as of insect and 'pest' life.

A bare branch in the evening could carry leaves and a bud in the morning and a flower by noon. But by evening the flower and leaves could have been demolished by insects—or sometimes by snails which came in waves, like an army, across the fields.

In the winter, when, for a short time, the vegetation was quiescent, there was a feeling that the land was impatient and could hardly wait for the spring, so that primroses and crocuses and violets were pushed out in January although February frosts could easily destroy them.

Provence was a master of the unexpected. The growth of plants and trees — and of insect and pest life—was explosive.

Against this restless background there were happenings, often with a comic flavour, although sometimes the comedy was black.

One day a pretty girl turned up at the *mas* with a young man in tow. I recognised her. She worked at the Tourist Office where I had been from time to time. She introduced the young man as her fiancé, but she didn't tell me her own name. She said: 'Do you mind if I just look at the *mas*?' and stood on the terrace, gazing at the old house, then turned to the garden and walked for a few moments among the olive trees and cypresses.

I was taken aback. What was all this about? She returned to the terrace.

'You see, this is really *my* house,' she said, by way of an explanation.

'*Your* house?'

I was mystified. I had bought the house in the normal way, with solicitors, documents, deeds, the transaction registered at a government office in Aix-en-Provence, from Monsieur and Madame Belmond. They, in turn, had bought it from my nearest neighbour, farmer Mabeille.

The girl repeated, 'Yes, this should have been *my* house.' She sighed. 'Thank you.'

I would have liked to understand what she meant, but before I could enquire further she held out her soft little hand to me, smiled in a meaningless way and went back to her car, the young man following. They drove away. Later, I went over to Madame Corbet, my neighbour.

'That girl from the Tourist Office was here,' I told her. 'Who is she? She says my house is really hers.'

Madame Corbet knew at once what I was talking about.

'Oh yes!' she said. 'She's the daughter of one of the Mabeille brothers—not your neighbour, not the one who sold the house to the Belmonds. Her father doesn't live on the farm. Yes, they do say something about your house. When the old man died—old Père Mabeille—there were quarrels in the family about the inheritance. It seems he wasn't very precise—old Père Mabeille—in his will. Guy— that's the girl's father—insisted that your house should really have gone to him. It was a drama among the brothers . . .' She smiled, a

42

vague smile meant to reassure—but I was anything but reassured. Was I to find out that I didn't after all own my house? 'No, no,' said Madame Corbet. 'In the end it was settled. But that girl, she still thinks the house should have been hers. That's what her father must have told her. If he'd inherited it, he might have given it to her.'

I found this incident disturbing. It was followed by other incidents and other happenings, unexpected, strange. These, together with the animals at Mas des Chats, kept me forever on the *qui vive*, often with a quiver of apprehension, an anxious wondering, 'Whatever next?'

10

—◇—

He had had a terrible winter, cold and starving, journeying hopelessly and dangerously along the roads, scavenging in the fields, like all lost and abandoned dogs. People had shouted at him, thrown stones, beaten him with sticks. He looked like an old, old dog, with his hind legs buckling under him, back bowed, raw and bleeding. And his eyes were full of pain.

So, by chance, in a pitiable state, he came upon the Mas des Chats.

I saw him in the distance. He kept well away. Old brown dog, I thought, hungry—surely he belongs to someone in the neighbourhood. But he was homeless, a vagrant traveller.

I made a dish of food and put it down on the edge of the field. He saw me do this but wouldn't take a step forward as long as I stood there, although he was famished.

I went back to the house. A little later the plate was empty and the dog gone.

Next day—and every day—he returned. He circled round the *mas*, always keeping his distance. He ate what I put down for him only when I'd disappeared.

Each day I saw him, bitter winter days.

He came nearer to the house but kept well away from me.

I fed him.

One day, I put his food on a step on the terrace. I watched from a window. He began to eat hungrily. Then, to my and his dismay, the dish fell from the step as he licked it vigorously, turning face down on the food. I couldn't go to help him because he would run as soon as he saw me—and he did go, after trying in vain to move the dish off the food.

Thereafter, he put a firm paw in the dish while he was eating, so as to restrain it and prevent it escaping. So then I knew it was the brown dog who had eaten food I'd put out if there was a paw print on the dish.

Sometimes he joined the gang of hungry dogs who roamed around, hunting food. More often, he was alone.

He circled nearer. When Monsieur Mercier made a fire to burn fallen leaves and branches pruned from shrubs and trees, I saw the dog lying in the embers to warm his thin, tired body. When the pale sun of winter shone he would stretch out against the cypress hedge in a nest he had dug himself in the dried cypress leaves. As soon as he saw me, he would stagger to his feet and limp away. Once I saw him hurrying triumphantly along the little road with a dry crust of bread in his mouth, hoping to eat it in some secret place before the other dogs could snatch it from him.

I grew fond of him.

I expected to see him every day.

I was anxious for him if he didn't turn up.

Then there were three days when he was missing.

On the evening of the third day, I stood at the kitchen door looking out to the garden before I closed the shutters. There, in the dark, I saw the old brown dog again. He seemed more terrified of me than ever, hiding in the bushes, waiting. I put down a dish of food for him, good, nourishing food with some meat and milk in it, and went away.

He came out haltingly, put his nose into the bowl and began to eat hungrily. But when he saw me standing at the cat window, he raised his head, staring with half-closed eyes until he was sure I wouldn't move.

When he had had enough—and he could only eat a little—he shambled away. I realised that one of his front paws was very swollen and painful. As his back legs were in any case weak he was forced to put his weight on the bad leg. So, wincing, he struggled along pathetically as best he could.

He went up the steps, over the bridge across the stream, hesitated and limped on up the hill.

Where on earth was he going? In the morning there was no sign of him. I pictured him hiding somewhere with his pain and his hunger and his fear. Perhaps he would return after dark.

I couldn't imagine what had happened to injure him so, and fervently hoped he had not been damaged by a vicious man. But he was so afraid of me, so terrified; in fact, it was clear he had been abominably treated by human beings. I longed for him to stay somewhere near the *mas* instead of going back to a place where he might be chased, stoned and tormented, with people perhaps trying to get rid of him.

It was clear that the brown dog had been abominably treated by human beings.

To my relief he was back the next day, the swollen paw a little less painful.

Gradually he grew to understand that I wasn't out to hurt him. Watching the Mas des Chats as he did from the distance he considered safe, he saw that I, the cats and Caramel took a daily walk in the vineyard if the weather allowed it.

There came a day when he decided to join the walk. Timid, hesitant, limping, he came along at the end of the line of cats. I was very pleased.

But on the return journey, the procession of cats passing through a clump of pines, one of the cats, probably Katy—or Sugar—decided to jump at him.

I heard him scream.

Even the lightest touch on his raw skin must have caused him agony. I was furious. One step forward and two back should, I thought, have been the house motto at Mas des Chats for the wilder animals.

But he had courage, that brown dog, and he was persistent. Very slowly, after many weeks of testing, he joined the household at Mas des Chats.

First he found himself a corner at the filter house by the swimming pool, where he slept on a chair mattress he had stolen. I added old towels and moved his bed into a sheltered corner. There he slept, and lay at times in daylight, gradually becoming more trusting.

One day, weeks later, he came up to me when I was walking in the fields and suddenly stood on his hind legs, placing his two front paws on my arm. He then sat down and handed me first one paw, then the other.

After that, it was only a matter of time before he was a dog of the house, a proprietor, with duties. He barked at strangers. He welcomed friends.

'You must give him a name,' said Monsieur Mercier who had taken to the brown dog, although the dog would not at first go near him. 'Here in France we have a custom for giving dogs their name. Every year there is a letter of the alphabet. The dogs of that year are named with words beginning with that letter.'

He didn't know the letter of that particular year but he advised me to go to the vet where a list of names and the letter would be displayed. I went to the vet and sure enough there was a chart hanging on the wall. The letter was 'I' and there was a long list of names beginning with 'I'. I read:

Ice cream, Idomineo, Impossible, Ivry, Imperator, Imperatrice, Ideal, Impeccable, Ibis, Idiome, Igloo, Imperial, Impetueux, Impulsif and Innocent.

There were many more. Not one name seemed suitable for the brown dog. I said to Monsieur Mercier, 'What name would you give him?'

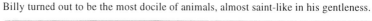

Billy turned out to be the most docile of animals, almost saint-like in his gentleness.

He put down his spade and said, in a slightly embarrassed way, 'Just after the war, I had a dog I loved very much. I called him Beelee. At the end of the war there were a lot of soldiers here—English soldiers. We heard English names. I often heard the name Beelee. I called my dog Beelee.'

'Right,' I said, and Monsieur Mercier was pleased, 'the dog is called Beelee.'

So the brown dog was Billy and he quite quickly learned his name. I did, in fact, call him Beelee when I spoke to him and when I shouted at him for misbehaving—on a walk, for example.

He turned out to be the most docile of animals, a soft, sweet, sensitive creature almost saint-like in his gentleness. Caramel loved him at once. She bullied him and fussed over him and jumped on him, in love and jealousy, and he took his cue from her.

So there were two dogs and eight cats of the household at Mas des Chats.

11

Brilliant, the huge old dog belonging to my farmer neighbours, the Mabeilles, had always been a frequent visitor to the *mas*. After some time I noticed that he had developed a great weakness of his hind legs. Once lithe and swift, a marathon runner of a dog, now he could only shamble along, relying on his two strong front legs to carry him.

If he lay down he had severe difficulty in getting up again. The farmer's son, young Louis Mabeille, whom I met by chance at one of the little bridges over the stream, told me there were times when Brilliant had to be helped to his feet. That was never the case when he visited me, which he still did—although less regularly than before—expecting a dish of food.

He appeared at almost any time of the day, staggering rather uncertainly down the bridge leading from the *colline*—to the consternation of any cats who happened to be on the terrace. Once, after rain, he fell, slithering to the ground on the wet, slippery stones.

By chance, I saw this accident from a window of the house. I rushed to help him. But by the time I reached him he had already hauled himself up onto four feet again, tottering round to the back of the house where he was used to receiving his food.

Nowadays, when he arrived, he tried to remain standing while waiting for his dish, since getting up was such a struggle. But if I was out and he realised he had a long wait ahead, he would lie down patiently among the wild persimmon trees. As soon as I saw him I would hurry out with his food and put his dish between his front paws. When he had eaten the last crumb he would hoist himself up and make for home, feeling satisfied and passing a little water on a convenient lavender bush as he went.

Being close to Brilliant was always a half-alarming, half-enjoyable experience. He was so big and heavy he was hardly credible. There was an intensity, almost a violence, in the fervour with which he wolfed his meal. His coat was often tangled with burrs and thistle heads which were only removed by his owners from time to time. And he smelt, sometimes, of stables and manure—an unkempt peasant dog, a rough, earthy dog.

In spite of his appearance he was a gentle and timid animal, anxious to please and obedient to command. On feast days and holidays, the children in the Mabeille clan put ribbons and garlands round Brilliant's neck and twined his collar with artificial flowers.

One day, a kind of dachshund turned up with Brilliant. His owners had taken on a second dog. The new dog was heavier and taller than an ordinary dachs. He wore a red collar and had an anxious expression. I discovered he was called George. He, too, was hungry. He tried to pick up any crumbs which Brilliant might have left in his dish. But Brilliant left no crumbs.

When George seemed very hungry indeed, at weekends in cold weather, when his owners were out for most of the day, I put out a dish for each of these dogs.

The cats got on well with George. He was nervous of cats and they realised they had the upper hand.

12

I don't remember exactly when Lily chose to withdraw from the hurly-burly of life in the kitchen at Mas des Chats.

'Chose' is perhaps the wrong word. Lily was driven by her instincts and her emotions, not her reason. Between one day and another she abandoned the cat window and the garden and the rosemary bushes in which she used to bury herself, hidden from human eyes, and retreated upstairs. She must have felt safer with the stairs between her and the real world. She established herself in a small suite of rooms. The main one, the one in which she spent most of her time, her *salle de séjour,* was large and light and pleasant, south-facing, so that the sun poured in and the moonlight at night. There she lay on a plastic sack of old letters which I had gathered in order to throw away. But she made this her bed before I could remove them and I didn't have the heart to dislodge her.

Instead, I covered the sack with a large towel, pale in colour to enhance her beauty. Dreamy Lily lay regally, seeming calm and relaxed—although she became agitated and hysterical at the drop of a hat.

She reminded me of Queen Victoria mourning the loss of Albert— and in fact her general demeanour was queenly because Lily, for all her strangeness and her madness, was what, in old-fashioned terms, was called a 'lady'. Fussy and feminine, she raised her eyebrows at coarse and brutish behaviour on the part of the other cats, shrank back with little cries of dismay if jostled and was, on the whole, dignified and gentlewomanly.

I clearly remembered the day I had found her and Rosie and taken them home from an RSPCA hostel in a Hampshire village.

'I'd like to adopt two kittens but they must be females,' I had told Mrs Campbell who ran the hostel, when I telephoned beforehand.

They were to be the companions of the male cat, Mews, at Ashford Cottage nearby. We went slowly round the various cages of rescued cats.

'A pity Mr Richards is out,' said Mrs Campbell, 'he would know which ones are female.'

Fussy and feminine, Lily raised her eyebrows at coarse behaviour on the part of the other cats.

Mr Richards was the vet who lived next door. But he was out on his rounds.

'*This* one,' cried Mrs Campbell, 'is *definitely* female.' She opened the cage where little Lily sat immobile and took her out. 'Everything about her says female.' Mrs Campbell was quite sure.

'If you're really certain . . .' I hesitated.

'I'm positive!'

She was not quite certain about Rosie, the second cat to be adopted.

'Bring her back if she turns out to be a male,' she said cheerfully. 'Take them to see Mr Richards. It's very hard to tell their sexes at this stage. But about the white one, I'm sure.'

Lily continued to be all feminine into her old age. When she established herself in her *salle de séjour*, I could easily imagine lace handkerchiefs and the smell of lavender, as Lily washed her coat to shining whiteness.

This room had been the hay loft in the days when the Mas des Chats was a working farm, with a horse to plough the fields. The hay was drawn up by a pulley to be stored in Lily's room. The room had a high, wide window which stretched from ceiling to floor. My predecessors at the *mas*, who had restored the place to its comfortable state, had sealed the lower half of the window to prevent accidents.

I used the room as a work room. There was a table with typewriter and shelves full of books. The painter, when I moved into the house, dignified the room by calling it the *bibliothèque*.

The rest of Lily's suite consisted of a place beside the radiator in the bathroom opposite the *bibliothèque*, the space under a double bed in a nearby spare bedroom and the flat rooftop leading out of the bedroom. She ventured out on the rooftop to breathe the scent of rosemary and cypresses which grew below. Becoming daring, she climbed carefully onto the roof tiles where she had a better view. Lily used the rooftop in summer only. She went under the bed at the slightest disturbance—the sound of the arrival of a strange car, an unfamiliar person entering the house, the crash of thunder . . .

The bathroom radiator provided winter warmth. There was a low stool beside it covered with a towel, making a tent for Lily's convenience. Here she lay in greatest comfort. I could often hear her

Lily used the rooftop in summer only. She would climb carefully onto the roof tiles where she had a better view.

musical snores when I went into the bathroom, as she soundly slept. She felt safe and protected there, although that didn't stop her rushing under the bed nearby at dangerous moments.

In her younger days, when she took fright, which was not infrequently, Lily would make a dash for the cat window, sail out onto the terrace and fly to some untraceable refuge. She would hide in thick bushes or halfway up the tall maple beside the little bridge over the stream. At least I could see her in the maple tree, but its trunk was smooth and large; there were no branches on its lower half. Lily found it difficult to come down and sometimes needed help. In the other places where she hid she was invisible. She was always slow to return to the house, even when the danger was long past. In very unfavourable weather, rain or sub-zero temperatures, I used to try to find her, to help her to return. I used to spend hours calling her, searching and calling. Even if starving or frozen, Lily would not return alone if, quite illogically, she still felt threatened.

Sometimes Marcelle, the *femme de ménage* at that time, a square, gentle, blue-eyed woman, would help me. We would go round and round the garden in different directions, each calling 'Leelee', she in her thin, sweet soprano, I more stridently and irritably.

There were times when I was searching for Lily at midnight or later, in pouring rain, shining torches into the cypress trees, under the laurel hedges, exhausting myself futilely.

In the end, we would find her, of course, or she would finally appear with pine or cypress needles in her coat. She looked composed; I was the one who was agitated. My neighbour Robert, a young Frenchman who gave all his animals, dogs and cats, the names of wines, had a white cat, slimmer and smaller than Lily, called Fleurie. He believed that white cats are particularly nervous because they have no camouflage. Certainly Lily's brilliant white coat was radiant in Provençal sunlight— and in the dusk, when white flowers are luminous.

But once Lily was established upstairs, her refuge was under the bed and there, too, she insisted on remaining for hours, long after the threat was removed. Her body was too heavy for her now stiff little legs and she hobbled awkwardly, although she could still put on a considerable turn of speed when she believed it was necessary.

Sadly, it became obvious she had no intention of returning to the garden. 'I'm too old,' she seemed to say. 'Gardens are for the young. One can have enough of country life . . . ' I was troubled that Lily felt she must give up the flowers and earth she had loved so much and the grass and the rain, but it was clear that, even in cases of extreme emergency, her instinct for self-preservation prevented her from rushing out of the cat window into the garden.

One night there was an incident with the new dog, Billy. Billy was the gentlest of animals and was more afraid of the cats than they were of him. Even Lily eventually came to realise this. But before she had understood that he was harmless, she was afraid. Late one night I heard the sound of pounding footsteps in the corridor and went to see what was happening. Lily and Billy must have startled one another. Both were racing neck and neck towards the stairs, each terrified of the other. My heart sank. I was sure Lily would end up in the dark garden. I hurried after them, together with a procession of cats roused from peaceful sleep.

I saw Billy easing his way out of the cat window—he was slender enough to make his entrances and exits in this way. Of Lily there was no sign. I went outside and began to call her.

Out of the house came the cats and Caramel, all thinking I was playing some mad but delightful game. I searched everywhere.

'Lilee . . . Lilee . . .' I used the high-pitched voice she sometimes responded to.

No sign of Lily.

Darkness and silence. The torch beam fell on bush and tree, into the cypresses, under the rosemary.

No Lily.

It was a freezing night. This was the first time she'd been out of doors for many months. She would catch cold. Her rheumatism . . .

In the end I came upstairs again, with the unreasonable hope that she had returned indoors on her own account. Lily was sitting comfortably on her towel, buffing her nails. She glanced at me casually and continued her *toilette*.

'Where *have* you been?' that glance enquired.

She hadn't leapt out of the cat window, she hadn't even gone down the stairs. She had veered off the corridor into a spare bedroom at the top of the stairs and there dived under the bed. While I called and searched in the garden she had quietly returned to her room. I understood only later what her tactics had been from watching her on other occasions when she took fright. She would, in fact, do anything rather than go out in the garden. I had seen her, when upset by a noise or a stranger, run down the stairs and then immediately up them again.

She was right. She was no longer nimble enough to escape the hungry dogs which ranged through the garden searching for food.

She might, of course have made little excursions into the kitchen and other downstairs rooms if it had not been for her inability to relate to the other cats. Lily was a loner. Her only real contact had been with Mews, the ginger tom in Hampshire.

57

Her only real contact had been with Mews, the ginger tom in Hampshire.

Now her only contact with another living creature was with me.

I took Lily's meals to her on a tray: little saucers which I set down beside her, long-life cream, mixed with water—and grass. She loved to nibble a few strands of young grass, preferably dried. Sometimes other cats of the household did join her in her room for a while. Oedipus, returning from his journeys abroad, might pass the night in the basket chair, which Lily never used. Or Hélène liked to be in a cat basket which I had put on the table for Nero when he seemed to be searching for a place to sleep. Nero had let me know he didn't care for it, but Hélène was pleased to find it.

It seemed to me that Lily would have preferred to be on her own and she tried to pretend, I think, that the visitors were invisible. Hélène equally pretended, from the look of her, that she was alone in the room. But perhaps the presence of other cats was mysteriously comforting.

Every evening I brushed Lily and combed her snowy coat, light and soft as goosedown. And while I brushed I talked to her. This quarter of an hour or so of daily contact was extremely important to her; she enjoyed every moment of it. The brushing took place just before I went to bed. Sometimes it was midnight, sometimes one or two in the morning, but I made a point of brushing and combing her without fail. She waited anxiously for this ceremony. Sometimes she was impatient and clawed the carpet. She began to purr as soon as she saw me pick up the brush and comb, and hurried to place herself on the plastic sack in the position she thought most favourable for the brushing.

I brushed and I talked and Lily listened and purred.

I talked of old times—of times she and I alone had shared, since Rosie was dead and the other cats were French.

I talked of Ashford Cottage, of Mews the ginger tom, of the animals that came out of the beech woods surrounding us, that Lily had known so well—the foxes and badgers and squirrels, the birds and the hedgehogs. I talked of Lily's favourite places in the garden, under the tree peony and the beech hedge, in the little pinewood, in the grass among the daffodils under the apple trees. I talked of Rosie, of the walks we used to take around the cornfield, Mews, Lily, Rosie and I progressing in single file.

All my memories of Ashford—all *our* memories, for surely Lily also remembered—returned at these times, and I knew there was a deep sadnesss in me which surfaced as I talked. I had loved that beautiful English place, and Lily I'm sure had loved it too. This was our bond.

Late at night Lily seemed to feel safe. She would totter out of her *salle de séjour* into the bathroom where I was taking a bath. There she would eat a few *croquettes* from a dish meant for universal cat snacks for those suffering from what the French call *les petites faims*.

Even Baby sometimes ventured upstairs to eat from this dish, although the biscuits it contained were identical with those in a dish in the kitchen. But Baby assured me by the enthusiasm with which she crunched the upstairs *croquettes* that they tasted much better than the others. Lily also preferred them to similar ones in her own dish in her room and she munched them happily when she came to see me in the bathroom. Then she would stretch, and scratch her face and lick her legs in a casual, happy-go-lucky way, without the nervous tensions of the day.

I talked to her and she responded with her little squeaks and cries to let me know she was listening.

––––––––––––––––◇––––––––––––––––

Hélène, too, wished to have a special relationship with me. Timid, sensitive, easily put out, she nevertheless persisted bravely in her attempts to get close to me. She was happy when we were alone together. In the late afternoon, she very often stayed indoors when I took the other cats on a walk in the vineyard.

She would then appear as it was getting dark and make it plain that she'd like me to take her into the garden. Because Hélène seemed so troubled and deprived, I did my best to respect her needs and reassure her when she was disturbed. Out we went together, she tripping along cheerfully.

We would reach the vineyard. By now the eastern sky, unearthly blue, was full of stars, while in the west the luminous colours of sunset, apricot rose and lilac, still stained a pellucid horizon. They were exquisite colours, made more intense by the solid wall of inky black cypresses at the foot of the sky.

Hélène and I would walk together as far as the vineyard.

Hélène skipped skittishly about in the cold air, sniffed the plants, emptied her bladder, stretched her long body against the trunk of a young willow tree beside the swimming pool, sharpened her claws and let me know she was grateful and ready to go indoors again.

13

A little house stood in the garden at Mas des Chats, next to the vineyard. It had two pleasant furnished rooms and a small terrace, was warm in winter, cool in summer. It was meant for *gardiens*, one man or woman or a couple who, in return for the comfortable lodging, would help with the care of the animals.

At one time, in the beginning of my life at Mas des Chats, I had thought it would be easy to find *gardiens*, but it proved to be extremely difficult. Over the years a series of French people occupied the little house, of all ages. All were unsuited to the job; some were particularly difficult and disturbing. The reason was, perhaps, that only fairly unstable people had applied for the job. After a number of failures, I decided to have, instead, British people to live in the little house.

They came out to Provence for a kind of holiday for two or three months at a time, helping me with the care of the animals and garden in exchange for the house. All those who came were agreeable and helpful but there were two couples I particularly valued—Sheila and John and Karen and Joseph. They were cheerfully involved with the animals, amused by them and caring of them. They entered with enthusiasm into the spirit of my mad household.

So now and then I had company and much laughter—but, because I didn't always find a couple to occupy the house, there were also many times when I was alone.

———◇———

All around the Mas des Chats the fields were abandoned. Once the older generation had given up working the land, retired—or died—there was no one to succeed them. It was a countryside in decay from the farming point of view.

My neighbour to the west, Monsieur Moret, once told me ve-hemently, 'My son isn't interested in farming. He's gone to work in a factory. And I am glad. Glad! Happy that he doesn't want to have the back-breaking struggle that I've had. Look at me!' And he thrust his bony, damaged hands under my eyes, pointed to his bent and twisted spine.

Many of the farmers in these parts were working small, uneconomic fields, perhaps with the help of their wives, doing the sowing and the planting and fertilising and spraying by hand and picking the crops by hand, bent over the furrows as in the paintings of a hundred years ago. The only difference between now and the last century was they had tractors instead of horse-drawn ploughs—and they had modern insecticides and fertilisers.

The physical hardships were enormous. Yet those who still farmed worked passionately, like Monsieur Moret and Monsieur Sabin, loving the land, loving to make the earth yield the crops, loving the abundant growth and the heavy harvests of Provence, loving their trees and their fruit and their glossy vegetables.

Once the lands were left untended, no longer ploughed and harrowed, the huge weeds thrived.

'But don't worry,' said my sister Nora cheerfully, 'quite soon the natural vegetation will take over. The land will return to its natural state . . .' Which meant scrub oak, wild lavender, rosemary, wild broom, gorse, pine woods, cistus . . . wild periwinkle . . . thyme . . .

14

—◇—

Oedipus was the messenger for the household cats, the ambassador, the troubadour. He carried the burden for the others of making contact with the wider, dangerous world beyond the garden, beyond the vineyard. He was more mysterious than the rest of the cats, driven entirely by instincts which were stronger than good sense or than his reluctance to enter the race.

He was a gentle, rather timid cat—or at least unaggressive. In spite of his size and strength he never picked a quarrel with the intruders at Mas des Chats. When the powerful males among the outside cats came prowling through the cat window, he stared and was uncertain and nervous—unlike Monsieur le Gris who tried to fight them off, howling and cursing. Within Oedipus' handsome body was a home-loving, comfort-loving gourmet, who still found his mother's support reassuring. But he was driven to go, north, south, east and west, in his search for what Monsieur Corbet called a fiancée. He was forced, in spite of himself, to take part in the often savage rituals of mating.

He would set off at a brisk wolf trot, to vanish into what might as well have been an Amazonian forest or the Sahara desert as far as I was concerned. Unless I supplied him with an electronic collar, I couldn't possibly find him.

Hours or days later he would return, spent, exhausted, starving, crying his strange cry as he came running across the fields. He would eat huge meals, rest a little, eat again, then off he went, out of the cat window and away. If he didn't return after two days I became anxious. Sometimes it was three or more, at the end of which I was strained and agitated.

I was very fond of him. He allowed me, after years when I couldn't get near him, to touch and caress him. And he came to greet me, if I met him in the vineyard or the garden, rubbing his strong young body against my legs, purring like an engine.

His affection and trust were deeply gratifying. I felt that Oedipus put me in touch with wildness—the creatures of the forest, the great cats, lion and leopard . . .

Within Oedipus' handsome body was a home-loving, comfort-loving gourmet.

So Oedipus had a double rôle. He linked the cats of the household to the wider world—and he was my link to the jungle.

15

He was tall and thin—exceptionally tall for a Moroccan, over six foot high—with a handsome head, almost bald, and fine features. In particular, he had a frank and charming smile. His name was Omar.

It was Madame Bartelli who urged me to take him as *gardien*, murmuring to me about him on the telephone in a soft, gentle voice, almost whispering.

'He's a good man,' she said, 'very, very good—an innocent, like a child—and pure, like a child. He is like a son to me, I love him as a son . . .

'What he needs,' her voice was like a buzz of bees on a summer afternoon, 'what he needs is quiet, somewhere peaceful, so that he can read the Bible and meditate. Where he is now it's impossible for him—in a dormitory, surrounded by Arabs . . . a different religion . . . noisy, dirty . . . whereas he is clean—so clean . . . you will see . . .

'There's only one thing,' she added. 'Once a month he will have a Visit. The Friends will come. About ten or twelve—they visit one another, each one has a visit from the others . . . But the visit is short, just for support and companionship . . .'

So Omar came to live at Mas des Chats for a while, supposedly to act as a *gardien*.

The situation had come about in the following way. It was in the days when I was still hoping to find that purely mythical figure—a responsible or reliable person or couple to live in the little house in the garden, rent free and all running expenses paid. In exchange he—or they—would give me a little help in the garden, watering the terrace pots in summer, for example, and a little help in looking after the animals.

It so happened that I mentioned my search to two young firemen when they came to rescue a cat—not one of mine—which had become stranded on the roof. One of them, Madame Bartelli's son, said he would think about it and let me know. His mother, he believed, knew of someone . . . a long story, to do with religion. His mother was a Mormon, and the person she had in mind was a Mormon also . . .

I gave Omar the small guest room which opened on to the terrace.

And that was how young Monsieur Bartelli brought Omar for an interview and tea one Sunday afternoon in early summer. Omar was dressed in his best clothes—a sober T-shirt and an ill-fitting tweed jacket which I urged him to remove as it was a hot afternoon. He wore shiny, thick-soled shoes and clean, neat trousers, slightly threadbare.

Young Monsieur Bartelli wore a sparkling white shirt, freshly ironed, impeccable, clean jeans and Italian leather sandals. We all drank tea on the terrace and discussed the possibility of Omar coming to live at Mas des Chats as *gardien.*

Omar seemed rather uncomfortable, I thought, and faintly reluctant. But he went through the motions of being keen on the idea and I rather liked him, although I had great reservations regarding his goodness and innocence as described by Madame Bartelli.

I decided against his occupying the little house and, instead, thought of giving him the small guest room which opened on to the terrace. A little wall in front of its door, covered with flowering plants, gave this room privacy. It had a lavatory, basin and shower of a luxurious kind. I furnished it with a small refrigerator, miniature oven and hot-plate for cooking. The bed was very comfortable. Although small, it was an attractive room.

Omar worked on an apple farm many kilometres away. He had no means of transport, so young Bartelli loaned him his ancient Lancia car, to my surprise. But Omar was to pay the petrol and running expenses. Bartelli was obviously doing his utmost to help Omar—or was he really helping his mother?

'He needs to read,' she had softly told me, 'he needs to pray. He finds he can't do this in that noisy place with all the other people and their different religion . . .'

The apple farm was an enormous concern. Omar and his fellow Moroccans did all the physical work—planting, spraying, picking, pruning, driving tractors, packaging. They were housed in large dormitories, bought their food in the nearby village, or ate in cafés there.

Great container transporters came from all over Europe to load apples to drive them back up the motorways—to Scotland, Scandinavia, Germany, Belgium—all the northern countries prepared to eat Golden Delicious and Elstar and Royal Gala . . .

It would take Omar about forty minutes to drive the old Lancia from Mas des Chats to the apple farm and return morning and evening. He had to start work at half-past-six in the morning, which meant a very early rise. But he had agreed that he wanted to come to Mas des Chats and so we settled on a date about three weeks ahead.

The three weeks became four, became five, became six. Omar kept delaying his arrival. I frequently wondered, did he really want to move? Madame Bartelli telephoned often and gently insisted on how much Omar wanted and needed to have his own privacy, his space. He appeared eventually and stayed one night. A few days passed. Then he brought his sparse belongings.

On each visit he gave me, as a gift, a large bag of sticky, inedible cakes. Each time he told me that next time he would bring even better ones, the real thing, really good, delicious cakes. He seemed troubled, nervous, on edge. I urged him not to bother to bring cakes or any other gift. I was happy to have him live in the room and would do my best to make him comfortable.

Finally, he settled in—that is, he regularly spent a few short hours sleeping at Mas des Chats, rose before daylight, chugged off in the Lancia and returned as darkness fell. He had no time at all to do anything to help me, but in order to fulfil his part of the bargain, I'd find him watering the garden at 10 or 11 p.m. in deepest night.

There *were* days when he came home—if home it could be called—earlier. I talked to him. How had he become a Mormon? I wondered, although I refrained from asking this directly. But he told me spontaneously.

It was Madame Bartelli who had found him (how? where?), rescued him, converted him to the Mormon religion. He was very indebted to Madame Bartelli. Both she and her husband (who was not a Mormon) had greatly helped him.They had legalised his living in France and had found him his job on the apple farm. He was an unhappy, restless man, poor Omar. It turned out that he had a wife and children in Morocco, but he never wanted to return there. By law he had to send two thousand of his four thousand earned francs to his wife each month, but she was living with another man (about this he was vague and uncertain).

Then the days when Omar returned home at a reasonable hour became fewer and fewer. Even at weekends he was not to be seen at Mas des Chats. There seemed to be little opportunity for him to read the Bible and pray and be at peace with himself.

I went and peered into his room through the glass door. Inside I saw chaos, a dishevelled bed, clothes scattered on the floor, food here and there, confusion.

The next time I had a chance to see him I said, 'Omar, I don't think you really want to be here. I think it's Madame Bartelli who wants you to be here. You'd be much better off on the apple farm, not having to do the journey twice a day . . .'

A great smile broke out on Omar's face. He patted me gently on the arm with an elegant, bony hand.

'You are a very clever woman,' he said kindly, 'you are very wise.'

And he laughed happily and we agreed that as soon as possible he should leave Mas des Chats and return to the dormitory. He was immensely relieved. It turned out that the old Lancia was extremely heavy on petrol. This expense was a great burden to him. But how to tell Madame Bartelli? I said to leave this to me. I telephoned her. I explained as tactfully as possible.

'He finds the journey difficult and tiring.' He had to get up so early, came home so late, no real time to help in the garden . . .

She laughed a little, sadly . . . but forgave him. Told me once more how good he was, how pure, how like an innocent child . . . She felt for him as a son.

And so Omar eventually gathered together all his few belongings— this took a while—and was installed again at the apple farm. His little room was not left in a very clean condition but this was understandable.

He returned to visit me every now and then. Now it was the autumn. The apples were being gathered.

On his visits, which were unexpected, unheralded, Omar brought enormous quantities of second-grade apples, those which were not fit for packing, which the workers could have free. He always announced himself with his splendid smile, saying, 'You are my father and my mother, my family, and so I come to visit you . . .'

He believed that, somehow, I might have some influence in high places to help him. But I had no such influence. What he really wanted was to go to Canada, or Australia.

'Canada preferably,' I suggested. 'They talk French there and you can't talk English.' The difficulty was to get permission to work there, an entry permit, a work permit, a permit to stay. He had heard of a man who, for a large sum of money, could arrange it. I advised him strongly against paying any man to arrange anything. The man would steal the money and he'd have no permit. Omar unhappily agreed this was possible. The French Government allows Moroccan workers who are not French citizens to come to France for nine or at most ten months of the year. Then they must return to Morocco. Before coming back to France they must report to the French consulate in Morocco and have a medical check—and so obtain a certificate vital for re-entry. At the end of his term of work at the apple farm Omar would have to go back to

Morocco. He was desperately against this and begged me to help him to stay in France.

I drove over to the apple farm. It was two o'clock. The Moroccan workers, a rough lot, were assembling, getting into lorries and vans to be driven off to various parts of the farm for the picking of the apples. They looked remarkably like a gang of slaves—except that they were there voluntarily, having no means of earning a livelihood in their own country—but, nevertheless, being paid the minimum legal wage. Omar, I could see, was some sort of head man, a team leader. He was delighted to see me. My presence raised his status greatly, it seemed. He called me 'Doctor' loudly, several times.

I spoke to the French overseer. Was there no way Omar could be helped or allowed to remain in France? None. By law he must return to Morocco for his few months there. Apart from obtaining a permanent *carte de séjour*, which was virtually impossible, he must go back.

Omar was desperate.

He would go underground again. He would marry a French girl. 'But you are already married . . .' He would divorce and marry a French girl—there were some who did this for the permission to stay . . . He would write to President Mittérand . . . If only he could have a job that lasted the whole year—a permanent job with people who would then apply for a work permit for him . . .

I knew a Belgian couple, two men, devoted to one another, who were looking for a *gardien*. They needed a man and wife—or two men—one to work in the garden, the other in the house.

I mentioned Omar as a possibility, at least to work in the garden.

Yves, the elder, turned the idea over in his mind, brooded a little. He knew of Moroccans who were capable of doing everything in the house, cooking, laundry, ironing . . . he was thinking perhaps of some silent and soft-footed manservant at one of the great hotels in Marrakesh or Rabat. I said nervously, remembering the state of Omar's room, that I didn't think Omar was like that, but I was sure he could work the garden—and be a reliable *gardien*. They would see him and decide. Poor Omar returned from the interview feeling offended and humiliated. They had asked him if he could make beds, do the ironing, cook.

Had he been less of a child, more shrewd, he might have said he could, been taken on and later resigned or been dismissed. At least he would have had a breathing space and been safe from the police.

He was possibly too nervous, over-sensitive to insults. But in a country where second-class citizens were often treated without any scruples as second-class citizens, and the war in Algeria was not forgotten, that was understandable.

Not long afterwards, he vanished. There were no more visits, no word. He had perhaps gone back to Africa as the law demanded—or perhaps was living in France illegally, hiding from the police.

Then I heard that Madame Bartelli—that disembodied pearly voice (I had never seen her)—had left her husband suddenly and gone to live in a Mormon colony in Marseille.

Did she take Omar with her?

He disappeared—as in a dream.

16

The *British Medical Journal* arrived regularly each week at Mas des Chats, neatly wrapped in its biodegradable, recyclable plastic envelope. It arrived when other mail could not arrive, delayed by postal strikes, blizzards or hurricanes. No matter what the weather or the state of the world, the *British Medical Journal* somehow got through and was there, magically, in the letter-box under the trees on the corner of the little road. Sometimes I opened it at once, sometimes I put it aside to be opened, perhaps, at another time.

This day, I began to read it. Katy, returning from a forage under a cypress hedge, saw me as I sat on a bench in the sunlight. She leapt on

I looked at charming Katy who had nestled down, purring.

my lap and began to purr. The page fell open at another article.

An eminent professor, Fellow of the Royal Society, was discussing the results of his experiments on cats, sectioning nerves here and there in the cat's body, examining the effects in due course.

I looked at charming Katy who had nestled down, purring louder.

Could the professor have sectioned the nerves on his own fireside cat, his Tibbles or Samson or Susie? I thought not. Somewhere far away, in the depths of a dreary, neonlit laboratory, an animal screamed, shrieked, cowered into the farthest corner of its cage, only to be dragged forward and mutilated yet again—helpless, suffering and alone.

Katy yawned, stretched her claws on my knees and sped away, singing as she went, The *British Medical Journal* fell to the ground, where I let it be.

17

Billy slowly recovered from the effects of starvation and cold and injury to his body, and he recovered also from fear and anxiety. It took time, but about six months after he had been accepted at Mas des Chats he was a changed animal, a rather handsome dog. Thick, wiry hair, ginger in colour, grew all over his body, and his limbs became stronger. He looked more solid and he was calm.

'He's a young dog', said the vet, Docteur Calan, on one of his visits to see a sick animal in the house. 'Not more than five years old, if that.'

Docteur Calan, one of the vets in Docteur Lamartin's large practice, was examining Billy's ear which had been discharging as long as he had been at the *mas* and which didn't improve in spite of ear drops and antibiotics of various kinds. 'There may be something in it which I can't see here. I must take him to the clinic and examine him properly.'

So Billy drove off with Docteur Calan, looking as though he was perfectly used to car travel, his nose in the air, gazing earnestly about him.

Three or four hooked and savage burrs were finally removed from deep inside his ear. Docteur Calan put them in a glass tube for me to see.

Poor Billy had other troubles before he became healthy and free of infections and parasites.

He once came back from a run in the fields covered with small round ticks which can kill an animal, so ferociously do they suck the blood of their host. The vet told me that every year several dogs do die (at the season when such ticks emerge and flourish), if they are very severely infested. On another occasion when Billy ran off on some excursion he came back covered with little wounds, probably made by pellets from a gun. He had one such wound on his knee which was swollen and painful.

The treatment he was given, antibiotics with cortisone, nearly killed him. We discovered he was allergic to cortisone. He had an acute crisis of irregular heart beat and abnormal breathing and it took some weeks

Once Billy felt secure at Mas des Chats he no longer went off on his own. His eyes, once black with pain, shone with happiness.

before normal rhythm returned. He was bred for hunting, I was told, with long spaniel-like ears and a long nose which could pick up a scent from a great distance.

A young man serving in the shoe-shop in Saint-Rémy, son of the proprietor and once a keen *chasseur*, told me Billy was a Fauve de Bretagne. The young man had a book on hunting dogs which he brought out to show me. There was a picture of a Fauve de Bretagne which Billy did, I thought, resemble.

But on one of our country walks I met an old man who had a genuine Fauve de Bretagne on a lead. He looked critically at Billy. 'Is he a Fauve de Bretagne?' I asked.

'Not really.'

'Has he got a bit of Fauve de Bretagne in him?'

'Not a lot,' he said kindly.

But that was before Billy's hair had become thick and curly, with moustache, beard and bristling eyebrows, characteristic of the Fauve. I didn't care what he was, mongrel or highly bred, except for the interest of it. He was a charming animal with a very good nature. Once he felt secure at Mas des Chats he no longer ran off on his own.

He had the sad, endearing habit, in his early days at the *mas*, of gathering a heap of little possessions together and keeping them as a secret store against a rainy day—pieces of dry bread, dog biscuits, cushions, coats, towels. He went often to sniff at his possessions to give himself a sense of security.

As he became a genuine member of the household at Mas des Chats, this habit largely stopped. But sometimes I would find a piece of bread, taken from the dish meant for hungry, roaming dogs, tucked into Billy's bed, or a toy, stolen from the cats.

His sleep became calmer. His dreams at first were nightmares, making him cry out in anguish in his sleep. Slowly, the dreams changed. He hunted, or at least ran, paws twitching, giving little squeaks of excitement.

And his eyes, once black with pain, shone with happiness.

As the weather grew colder, Sugar would warm herself on the radiator before coming cautiously across my bed.

My other new arrival, friendly Sugar, continued to be a warm-hearted and cheerful cat. She was exceptionally affectionate and the least jealous of all the animals, having such great confidence in her attractiveness, such a strong sense of self-value—the advantage of having been much cherished as a kitten, I concluded—although, of course, I knew nothing about her previous life.

In the early mornings, after a night of intermittent hunting in the garden, weather permitting, she came up to the bedroom. As the weather grew colder, she warmed herself on a radiator before coming cautiously across the bed, avoiding any other animal who might be sleeping there, and placed herself on my chest, purring loudly.

Occasionally she made a contralto remark, and stretched out a soft paw which she placed firmly on my mouth. Then she gave my face a good wash with her kind, rough tongue, made it clear she was fond of me, bit my hand delicately and retired to the radiator for a deep sleep. She spent the day sleeping and, at intervals, eating, so as to prepare herself for another night's efficient hunting. And if there was any time left over, she was pleasantly sociable with Baby, the only member of the female cats who wasn't jealous of her.

Monsieur le Gris, however hard he tried, could do nothing to shake her solid self-assuredness, which I envied and admired.

18

That autumn, many owls circled Mas des Chats, night after night. The first tentative call sounded like the cry of an animal, making me stop in my tracks to listen—a cat? A dog? Then came the long hooting notes, hollow and echoing. From tree to tree they went, calling with melancholy fervour.

In the autumn rain, the large toads also called to one another, a slow, silvery croak of deep satisfaction.

And the rains brought flowers into the fields and along the banks of the canals, acid yellow, egg-yolk yellow, white and mauve. White and pink daisies on long thin stalks sprang up in the grass.

The English primroses suddenly began to flower, innocent pale faces staring up. The weather, rough, cold and wet, must have seemed like an English spring.

Early one morning—a day of cloud and rain, then a spell of sunlight, with bright blue sky, then rain again—I heard the sound of strange barking—was it barking? More like the cry of a despairing camel, or some other groaning, weary creature—sheep or goat, but not a dog.

Then there was silence for a while, and then the sound was heard again—and again—and, after another pause, once more.

The cry seemed to come from somewhere in the vineyard. I went to look. Something was lying in the stream which ran alongside the vineyard, separating Mas des Chats from the Corbets' field. In the distance the thing in the stream seemed to be a large, pale creature, sheep or dog, trapped in the water and unable to move.

It turned out to be a large, drenched dog, an enormous old spaniel, wedged among big stones under a little footbridge, unable to move, to save himself by climbing up the bank on to hard ground. He stared at me from rheumy, perhaps blind eyes, the colour of blackberries, in a white face. At first, in his distress, he tried feebly to bite me, then understood that I wanted to help him up. There were difficulties. He was weak and massive. To free him, I had to remove the rotten planks and pieces of wood which made the footbridge. Then, using all my strength, I dragged him out, a dead weight.

The sun-drenched terrace at Mas des Chats was bright with a profusion of geraniums.

The garden was a cool, green haven for the animals.

As he grew older Nero's glossy black coat acquired a rusty look.

Monsieur le Gris—deeply insecure, by turns a bad-tempered bully and endearingly childlike.

Baby remained wild and lonely after her mother died . . . until she attached herself to Monsieur le Gris.

Monsieur and Madame le Gris—an ill-assorted but charming couple.

In her later years Lily decided to remove herself completely to the upper part of the house.

The enchanting Brown Sugar, utterly confident, her shining coat dappled and mottled like sunlight on fallen leaves.

As soon as he was on firm ground, he ran off—or rather, limped and hobbled, but moving fast, I saw him reach Madame Corbet's porch. There he lay down to rest. I would have taken him back to Mas des Chats, to shelter and food, but as soon as he saw me, he was off again, terrified.

Rain began to fall once more, heavily. He had disappeared and I went back to the house. Soon, I saw him again, circling the swimming pool. I put a dish of food under a bush and went away.

He ate ravenously and went back to the spot where he had fallen into the stream. There, the collie-like dog from the next door farm, a long-nosed, aristocratic, well-mannered animal, taking his daily stroll in our direction, found him. The poor old spaniel, now totally exhausted, collapsed on the wet ground. The collie, wagging his tail, inspected him carefully as he lay on his back, paws in the air. So I was able to grab hold of him and, holding his neck firmly, I piloted him to the small guest room on the terrace at Mas des Chats. He lay on the floor. He was at the end of his tether. He was certainly very old, white in the face, a huge, pale spaniel with long floppy ears. His coat was marked with flecks and spots of lightest chestnut. Deaf, too, I thought; and certainly very confused.

I dried him. I laid him on an old rug. I covered him to keep him warm. I gave him food and water. After he had eaten again he lay hardly moving, so exhausted he was. His ears were so tangled in burrs I had to take scissors to free them.

What next?

I sat down to consider.

I had to find his owner if I could. First, a call to the vet.

Yes, a woman had telephoned, a white dog with chestnut markings lost on the Orgon road. She had left a telephone number.

The telephone number belonged to a polite man in an insurance office, who knew nothing of lost dogs nor even women who might have called the vet.

The police also knew nothing of large, white, lost spaniels.

For a moment a sense of hopelessness came over me. Was I to be saddled with this great animal for the rest of his old life? He seemed too much of a burden in addition to all the other animals at Mas des Chats.

The corner of the stream beside the vineyard, where I found Oscar.

Then strength returned.

There would be a solution. There is always a solution.

I must make a plan—but first, a tour of the neighbourhood. It was just possible, although very unlikely, that someone knew something about him. Caramel and Billy leapt into the car and off we went.

My first call was to Madame Sarlat, up the road to Les Baux. She knew me from my earlier vain journeys in search of cat owners—or when I was searching for my own lost animals.

She was standing in her front garden, a lucky chance. We exchanged greetings and talked about our mutual friend, my neighbour Madame Corbet. Then I asked, did she know of anyone who had lost a dog round there? She said, suspiciously,

'What sort of dog?'

I described him: white, large, old, brown spots, a spaniel . . .

She listened carefully. Then she said, 'Long ears? Hanging down?' She gestured with her hands next to her ears to show the length of the spaniel's ears.

'Exactly,' I said. At this point I wondered if she was about to say she knew nothing of such a dog but, to my relief, she went on, then yes, if I was sure about the ears . . .

She paused again, then said, rather reluctantly, I thought, 'It's probably Oscar.'

'Oscar?'

'Madame Henri's dog.' Madame Henri had been round early that morning, asking if Oscar had been seen. He had disappeared during the night. 'Go down and ask them,' she suggested, and described where they lived.

We chatted for another moment, but I could hardly wait to drive at speed to the *mas* where Monsieur and Madame Henri lived.

On the way it occurred to me that Madame Sarlat had not seemed very pleased that Oscar had turned up. Perhaps, I thought, she and the Henris were not good friends.

Left at the cross-roads, first gravel road on the right; we had arrived.

A strange place—more like a zoo except that the animals in cages were all domestic ones: dogs of all kinds and all colours, ducks, geese, sheep, hens of many varieties and cockerels, rabbits . . .

Just as I reached the great lime tree which shaded a paved terrace at their front door, amidst a ferocious clamour of barking dogs, Monsieur and Madame Henri returned from their work in the fields, solemn-faced, staring with disquiet at this strange, smiling *étrangère*.

'I believe I have your Oscar,' I said cheerfully.

They seemed not to understand.

I tried again.

'You have a dog called Oscar?'

At once their faces became tense and anxious.

'Yes . . . ?'

'I have found him.'

Their faces changed—but, to my surprise, their expressions were of deepest gloom and sorrow.

'He is dead?'

'No, no. Not at all—very much alive.'

They could hardly believe me.

'He is alive?'

'Absolutely. I have him down at the *mas*.'

'He isn't dead?'

'No, not dead.'

When, early that morning, they had found that the old dog had disappeared, they had convinced themselves that Oscar knew his end was near and, according to the old notion, had taken himself off to die. They had this idea so firmly in their minds that it was quite hard for them to accept the opposite. But when at last they realised that Oscar was alive they were overwhelmed with excited happiness.

Oscar was their most loved and oldest pet.

They showed me his living quarters, a kind of cloakroom full of gardening tools opening out on to the terrace. They explained that the door had always to be left open because, in his old age, Oscar's bladder was weak and he needed to go out from time to time during the night.

The circumstances of his departure were described—but first they must explain that he had become not quite right in the head—a little demented—just his age—it happens to some old people.

Monsieur Henri then told the story. He had not slept well the night before. After turning round and round restlessly, he had left his bed to sit and read in the room just above Oscar's cabin.

It was about 3 a.m. He had heard Oscar come shuffling out—he assumed it was to empty his bladder. Then there was silence and he took it for granted that Oscar had returned to his bed.

But it must have been then that Oscar decided, in his demented way, to take a walk. Presumably, he had wandered off and kept on going. Eventually he had fallen in the stream where I found him.

At 6 a.m., the Henris rose and found Oscar gone. They had searched everywhere, gone round to the neighbours and finally decided that Oscar had taken himself off to die—because that is what old or sick animals, feeling themselves near to death, are supposed to do. Many of them perhaps do just wander off and end up in some sort of trouble from which they can't extricate themselves, being feeble and frail, like Oscar.

In any case, the Henris decided he was dead and had this idea so firmly planted in their minds they were already in deepest mourning for Oscar. We all set off at once to bring Oscar home, I and the two dogs in my car, the Henris in a small van bearing Oscar's rather threadbare mat and blanket.

Before we left I was given six newly laid eggs and three marvellously fresh lettuces.

When Madame Henri saw Oscar, tears ran down her cheeks.

She had brilliantly blue eyes and pretty features in a worn face. She and her husband must have been permanently exhausted by all the work involved in caring for the animals and also their fields where they grew vegetables for the market.

Oscar had hardly moved since I left him. Madame Henri knelt down and spoke to him, soothing his brow and hugging him.

Oscar didn't seem to recognise them. They got him to his feet and took him outside. There he stumbled around in circles, looking dazed. He couldn't hear them, of course, and perhaps could scarcely see or smell them.

They finally persuaded him to limp off to the van where they hauled him in to the back.

Madame Henri, still gently weeping, climbed in beside him. They thanked me many times. I could not know, Monsieur Henri told me, what an overwhelming pleasure I had brought to their lives. Beaming, he drove away. I waved. Caramel and Billy could make nothing of the entire episode. But I rejoiced.

19

My English cat Rosie had always taken the view that it was best to let the forces of nature have their way. The weak and unfit should be eliminated, according to the rules of evolution as proposed by Darwin. Only the strong and capable should survive. She led her life accordingly and tried to persuade me to accept what she considered was the inevitable—the triumph of instincts over reason. She worked hard to protect and preserve her territory, to get rid of those who tried to muscle in, to make sure that only the élite (and that meant her) ran the local government.

My own views were diametrically opposed to hers. I was always trying to persuade her to live and let live. I was always rescuing creatures that she would have had die. I was endlessly taking the household animals for medical treatment when they needed it, desperately trying to save them against all odds. That, I told Rosie, was the human contribution to the state of things, caring for and curing the weak and ill and fragile.

But even as I might have been proposing to her to accept these views, the violent sound of gunfire rocked the *mas*, volley after terrifying volley, coming from the fields between the cypress hedges nearby. The shooting was performed by the *chasseurs*, busily trying to eliminate the already impoverished bird life in the immediate vicinity.

Monsieur Mercier and I discussed the hunters in one of our many conversations about the state of the world. He was telling me how a migrant robin followed him about as he worked in his allotment, almost sitting on his boot as he dug the earth. He was sure—or at least fairly sure—that it was the same robin which came year after year to his field. A trusting little bird, he felt it was only there because it understood—or perceived—that he would not harm it. The same applied to the thrushes and blackbirds and other birds in his plot. He was the only man in the *Quartier des Jardins* who tried to preserve life and not destroy it. All around him men were putting tons of insecticide and other poisons on their tomatoes and lettuces and cherries and apricots. All around him, men were shooting the blackbirds and

Rosie had always seen herself as one of the élite.

thrushes and anything that moved—for the pleasure of shooting.

'When they've killed everything off and there's nothing left to shoot,' he said, 'they throw their hats in the air so as to have something to shoot at. They shoot butterflies—anything . . .

'Don't think,' he added, 'it's only the peasants and the boys with nothing better to do who are the hunters. It's the businessmen and the doctors and lawyers and members of parliament who go down to the Camargue and pay a thousand pounds a day because they love to kill. Human beings love to kill. To think anything else is *hypocrite* . . .'

And as he said this another volley of gunfire from the nearby fields shattered the air and my views on human compassion.

20

I took a walk every day with the dogs. Before the arrival of Billy, Caramel and I went together all over the neighbourhood. Many of our walks took us along the banks of the Canal des Alpilles, the largest canal of the area. The path was grassy, shaded in mid-summer, protected from the *Mistral* in mid-winter. We hardly ever saw anyone else except at the weekend.

On Sundays the Alpilles swarmed with walkers. 'Swarmed' is perhaps an exaggeration. There were many walkers and also cyclists. Sometimes people walked in groups, a club, perhaps, in one of the small towns of the region. All were dressed in richly coloured clothes made of windproof, water-repellant, modern fabrics, purple and scarlet, turquoise and yellow, aquamarine and petunia pink—and their care-fully designed shoes were made to match.

During the week, however, we usually walked alone; but one day, on a stretch of the canal where the water flowed deep and fast, we were overtaken by an elderly man with two very large and fierce black dogs. The owner, thin and fragile, wore a blue-grey beret and frayed jeans. He nodded a polite *Bonjour* and was about to pass us by when, to my horror, the dogs swooped down on poor Caramel with snarls and growls of menace. The little dog must have been terrified, but kept her head. She scooted down the vertical bank of the canal out of reach of the attacking dogs. There was a faint plop as she hit the water, but she scrambled out immediately and put herself—at the level of the water surface—in a hole in the bank, the home, perhaps, of a water rat. She was safe there but the great dogs hovered on the bank above her, still threatening her. Their owner began to remonstrate gently with them.

'*Kaa!*' he said to the female of the pair, the more aggressive of the two. '*Kaa! Ce n'est pas gentil! Un si petit chien! Ce n'est pas gentil, Kaa!*' In his efforts to reason with Kaa, he knelt on the bank and peered down, to meet Caramel's velvet-brown eyes just above water level. '*Il est si petit, Kaa! C'est ignoble!*'

Eventually he persuaded the pair to move on. They were about to set off when he stopped to make a graceful speech of apology. All I

It was a long time before Caramel wanted to walk along that stretch of the canal again.

wanted was to rescue Caramel, who by now must have been cold and shivery. They went. We watched them disappear in the distance.

After some persuasion, Caramel came cautiously out of her hole and climbed the bank. She shook herself vigorously and wagged her tail—a cheerful and resilient little animal. But it was a long time before she wanted to walk along that stretch of the canal again.

Another favourite walk was along a little road, the Mas de Verran, it was called, not far from Mas des Chats.

At one end of this road there was a hamlet, a huddle of very old houses, one leaning against another, looking medieval in their haphazard arrangement. Anyone living there was in very close contact with his neighbours. One couple had a tiny square of garden, just big enough for two deck chairs. In spring and autumn they sat in these chairs trying to catch an elusive sun, their knees touching the wire of their fence. In another house, an elderly woman kept two enormous barking dogs in a wire enclosure, or sometimes chained to a tree in her yard. When we passed by, they went into a frenzy of barking, hurling their heavy bodies about, looking savage and dangerous. Once they escaped and turned out to be meek and gentle, accompanying us on part of the walk.

Opposite the old lady's rather ramshackle dwelling was a more organised house in which lived a white, bright, bored little poodle. This dog and Caramel always had an enjoyable barking match, each jumping up and down beside the garden wall of the poodle's residence, or racing backwards and forwards shrieking and cursing one another until I persuaded Caramel to move on.

At the end of the hamlet was a crumbling, ancient *mas* in which lived a very old man. I used to see him sometimes if I walked that way in the middle of the day. He would be getting out of a car, having just been brought home by his son, at whose nearby house he had had lunch, and would be clutching a half or perhaps a third of a long loaf of bread—his supper and breakfast.

They fetched him every day, brought him home with his bread and drove away. I wondered if, like many old people, he preferred to live alone in his own place and his son respected his wishes.

They took good care of him, I thought, as much as anyone could. One day in winter when I met him, he was wearing a thick new cardigan, hand knitted—by his daughter-in-law, perhaps—in speckled blue wool. His shirt was clean and ironed. Below the waist, things had gone a little awry. His shabby old trousers were only half buttoned and that wrongly. The laces on his old farm boots were not properly tied and might have tripped him up.

When he got out of the car and saw me, he stopped and had a little talk, shading his stone-grey eyes from the sun, half-blind, perhaps. He asked me where I lived and I had to raise my voice for him to hear. He told me what a good lunch his family had given him. He was eighty-six years old. He took an interest in things. He grew a few flowers in an old horse trough in front of his house.

Next to the house was an ancient stone pillar with a metal cross on top of it. A straggling old rose grew beside it. I noticed one day that he had tied its disorderly branches to the pillar with a piece of string.

He hadn't much of a life there, alone in the old house at the end of the village—but such as it was, he enjoyed it. Caramel and I walked on and he waved goodbye.

———————◇———————

Sometimes we went along the avenue of planes leading to the clinic of Saint Paul, where Van Gogh had been a patient. The clinic was on a hill south of the town near the antiquities, the Roman arch and monument and the ancient town, Roman and pre-Roman, which was still being excavated.

There was a short road from the clinic gate to its buildings and garden, and to a church with an adjacent cloister. Irises grew in the garden beds beside the road and there had formerly been a small bronze head of Van Gogh on a stone pillar, which had been stolen one night and never traced.

All around the clinic and up into the Alpilles, the *Mairie* had signposted walks taken by Van Gogh and places where he had painted some of his most famous works. The spirit of the artist still walked there, his eyes still seeing through our eyes, since anyone familiar with his paintings saw the olive trees, the rocks, the Alpilles, the irises, as he had seen them.

The little cloister beside the church was exquisite. In between the charming curving pillars around the small square of interior garden, there were huge tubs of thriving aspidistras and geraniums.

Occasionally we followed the footpaths among the pine woods at the top of the main road across the Alpilles. There, in a large parking area, during the summer, fire engines were permanently drawn up, in a constant surveillance of the surrounding country. A fireman, always on the alert, watched for the first wisp of smoke heralding a forest fire.

The crews of the engines had elaborate meals among the pines, tables covered with cloths, bottles of wine and water standing among properly laid out knives and forks and glasses, for three-course

Walking in the pine woods was forbidden in the summer, but it was possible to walk up to the summit of one of the hills nearby.

lunches. The French certainly believed that ceremony at meal-times was important, no matter how *al fresco* the circumstances.

Walking in the woods was forbidden in summer because of the risk of people causing a fire, but it was possible to walk up to the summit of one of the hills nearby. There, enthusiastic bird watchers from all the countries of Europe came with telescopes and field glasses, and lay on the ground to observe the birds of the Alpilles.

One of my favourite walks was in the little town of Noves on the way to Avignon.

A narrow passage led up from the walls of the old town to the top of a hill—the rue du Château, although there was no longer any castle on the summit.

There, on a grassy knoll, a few pines stood, and all around there was a splendid view. The Mont Ventoux rose high above the plain in the north-east. To the south lay the chain of the rocky Alpilles, a long, irregular, sharp-edged stain of blue along the horizon. Below the hill-top were the roofs of the town, all shapes, all angles, covered with beautiful old tiles of russet, umber and grey, and here and there a church tower stood above them.

On a fine day the wind blew gently up on the hill and the air was crystalline. Caramel put her front paws on the low wall protecting the path from a steep drop on the brow of the hill and, breathing the clear fresh air, we both admired the view.

———————◇———————

After Billy had been at Mas des Chats for a while I took him with Caramel when we went on our walks.

Caramel was the perfect walker when she was in good health, trotting just ahead of me, keeping her eye on me, obedient to instructions. Billy in the beginning was wild, an incoherent walker, over-excited, rushing about, dashing ahead. For his safety I kept him at first on a lead. Gradually he settled down and began to understand what a walk was about.

Although he loved the country walks and would rush forward with a happy toss of his head, he preferred going to the town. He would investigate every smell punctiliously and with passionate interest. Caramel and I—she was more patient than I as she was so fond of him—often had to stand and wait until he was quite sure he had understood the import of some particularly remarkable scent. Then he would allow us to move on.

Between days of violent rain and days of bitter *Mistral*, there was a day of calm—mild, sunlit—when soft, sweet air floated up from the south across Provence.

I took the dogs walking in the flat stretch of land between the blue hills of the Alpilles in the south and the Montagnettes in the north.

To the north-east, the Mont Ventoux rose up out of the plain, its tall summit white with snow which had fallen on its chalky surface in the

Caramel was more patient with Billy than I was.

night. The mountain looked like the real Alps, white peak against the cornflower sky.

The two great canals were full of water which ran shining between green banks. Brilliant young grass had shot up with the heavy rains. The fields were ploughed and harrowed—a chocolate-coloured earth crumbled into neat lines, ready for sowing.

Two large white birds like egrets sailed out of the sky and landed in the middle of a field. Then a heron drifted across and sank down farther upstream. The dogs and I hurried along the little road, on and on, exhilarated, dazzled.

21

Messaline was a horse, a great grey mare of the Camargue, whom we found one morning tethered by a long chain to a stake in the field beside the vineyard.

The news was brought by Baby. The cats and I had strolled out in the early morning sunlight of an autumn day to walk around the swimming pool. Baby had ventured a little farther, passing through the cypresses into the vineyard. She came racing back, frightened and breathless, letting me know there was a drama in the field by the vineyard. I and Katy—she was always game for any adventure—went to see what the trouble was.

There, gazing at us calmly, raising her large head for a moment from the serious business of cropping such grass as she could find, was Messaline. To Baby she must, of course, have seemed a giant—and she was a particularly large and heavy example of a Camargue grey.

Katy and I approached her, but even Katy hung back from close contact with a creature as enormous as Messaline.

I couldn't remember whether Katy had arrived at Mas des Chats before or after the era of Jasmin, another Camargue horse who belonged to the nearest member of the Mabeille family, my neighbours to the north of Mas des Chats.

Jasmin had lived in a small field behind my *mas*. The resident cats and I had visited him daily, taking him bread and carrots. Then, one day, finding his field empty, we learned he had been sold to another member of the Mabeilles, Messaline's owner. For those cats of the household who had arrived after he had been taken away, getting to know a Camargue horse would be a new experience.

I could see at once that she was a gentle and charming animal. She was delighted to have me talk to her. It transpired she was extremely sociable, and used to enjoying company. To be all alone in a large field without any kind of shelter was, for her, uncomfortable and dreary. In no time I was spoiling her with carrots and bread.

At midday her owner turned up. He had come to see if all was well with her. He brought a small battered tin bath which was to be filled with water for her drinking supply. He had expected to find water running along the little canal which bordered the field. But the canal was dry.

In autumn and winter the canals were cleaned. The water supply was cut off most of the time. Messaline's water must be brought from another source.

I knew Messaline's owner. He had once owned a flock of sheep and two dogs which went with them. He used, at times, to graze his flock in the fields around Mas des Chats. But he found the work too hard, the financial reward too small. He sold his flock. Now he worked as a gardener for one of the hotels.

Messaline had been stabled in an open shed in the centre of a cluster of old farm buildings. She had a companion, another horse of the Camargue. I saw them whenever I walked by, eating their heads off, knee deep in hay and round as barrels. At that time I knew nothing about her, and only learned her name from her owner that midday when he came to visit her in the field. Messaline was a Roman name. I consulted the encyclopedia.

'Messalina, *c.* AD 26–48. Wife of the Emperor Claudius, mother of Britannicus and Octavia, who became Nero's wife.' Messalina seemed to have been a difficult and unhappy woman. Her name was, I thought, unsuitable for the Camargue mare who was good-natured and sedate.

She was seventeen years old, the shepherd told me. She had been with his family since she was a foal and they all loved her. The children, now grown up, used to ride her when they were young. She was '*douce, douce*'.

What about Messaline's supply of water? I offered the use of a tap near the swimming pool.

A polite acceptance, an expression of gratitude.

But the offer was never taken up. The shepherd went away. The tin bath was left empty, lying on its side in the rough grass. Messaline went to it and snuffled around it, trying to find a drink.

I filled the bath, lugging plastic cans and a bucket across the tufty grass.

Messaline drank like a vacuum cleaner, emptying the bath quickly, eager for more water. I gave her more. I kept the tin bath full.

A baffling situation developed. Over the next weeks, as long as she was tethered in the field, Messaline depended on me for her drinking water—and partly on me for her food. The grass in the field was coarse and sparse, growing among thick, inedible weeds. She rapidly munched up everything edible in the circle in which her chain allowed her to move. The stake to which she was tethered should have been shifted every day or two.

At first the shepherd came regularly to change her position in the field. Then, gradually, he turned up less frequently. Messaline grew hungrier and hungrier. She tried to escape from her chain. She was restless.

One day the shepherd tied her to a pillar on the side of the old ruined *mas* at one end of the field—a farmhouse which belonged to his sister, the gently mad Giselle Mabeille. In the morning, when I went out, I found Messaline slowly strangling herself by walking round and round the pillar, the chain which held her by a collar round her neck getting shorter and shorter.

I had to get hold of the chain firmly and force her to walk round and round the pillar in the reverse direction until the chain had unwound completely. But she might easily repeat the whole process and end up dead.

I was angry. It was stupid and dangerous to have left her tied to the pillar. And my anger over the shepherd's neglect of his horse and my having to stagger across the field with buckets of water now rose to the surface.

I telephoned him. I spoke angrily. I accused him of ill-treating Messaline. I told him he must come at once and release her from the pillar.

He came. Highly offended, he refused to talk to me. He undid the chain which held Messaline to the pillar and placed her stake in the field and there attached her.

I asked, 'Why didn't you visit her earlier? She almost strangled herself.'

'I couldn't have come yesterday,' he said huffily. 'I was out.'

'What was to happen to Messaline, then?'

'I've told you. I couldn't have come. I went out. To visit relations.'

There was no point in arguing any further.

I said, 'And what about her drinking water all these weeks? What did you think she would drink?'

At this, a very strange mixture of expressions came over the shepherd's face—expressions both shrewd and cunning but also enigmatic and stupid. He was silent. The expressions said, 'You and I know perfectly well you weren't going to let Messaline die of thirst.'

I decided I preferred to remain friendly with this close neighbour rather than have a feud.

I said, more mildly, 'Why did you bring Messaline here? Why didn't you leave her in her shed at the farm?'

He was still sulky, still muttering that no one could accuse him of ill-treating his animals. He looked after all his animals. Everyone knew that. Did Messaline look ill-treated? (Glancing at the benign Messaline, I had to admit her outward appearance was splendid.)

But then the shepherd explained that the shed where Messaline had been housed was no longer available to him—no doubt some quarrel in the Mabeille family—and that he had nowhere to stable the horse.

And he added with that same cunning, shrewd, silly expression that he thought he would have to sell her. Hay was so expensive, he couldn't afford to keep her. Perhaps he wouldn't be able to find a buyer at her age. She might have to end up at the butchers . . .

I said, 'Do you really mean you want to sell her? Because I have friends who might be interested in buying her.'

Yes. He thought so.

The outcome of this encounter was that, not long afterwards, a field became available to the shepherd next door to his house. This he enclosed and Messaline was moved there—close enough to the family to be fed and watered regularly, I hoped.

Then I learned that a friend of mine was looking for a horse for her child, a calm, stable, elderly horse exactly like Messaline. I put her in touch with the shepherd. She telephoned him.

He wanted to sell Messaline, yes. Later, after all he didn't want to sell Messaline. Later, yes, perhaps he did. It depended on whether another of his horses was sold or not and this depended on a grandmother's disapproval of her grandchild being given a horse and finally, 'No, he didn't want to sell Messaline. His children loved her too much. They didn't want him to sell her . . . a family horse, you understand. She's been in the family all these years . . .'

So Messaline stayed with the shepherd and lived in the field by his house.

'And what became of Jasmin?' I asked, since it was to the shepherd that Jasmin had been sold.

'Ah, Jasmin . . .' and again that strange expression. Jasmin had been sold and, he thought, was now working with the *taureaux* . . .

I enquired no further. I hoped that charming horse took part in Provençal bullfights rather than Spanish *corridas*. In the Provençal version, the bull is not killed and the horses are not usually injured. The game is to snatch a white cockade from the horns of a bull. Perhaps Jasmin had a good owner who was fond of him. He deserved one.

The cats and I missed Messaline in the field beside the vineyard. We had become accustomed to our daily visits to her, treading across the heavy tussocks of tough grass, pushing through tall, dry weeds. They watched, gathering around, as I gave Messaline her water and carrots. They learned not to be alarmed by her.

Her strong sculptured shape added beauty to our landscape. On cold foggy mornings steam came from her nostrils and mouth, merging with the soft general mist which drifted across the fields towards the shadowy hills. On windy days, when the sky was an Alpine blue and the outline of the hills knife-sharp, Messaline tossed her mane and stamped her great feet. Noble and statuesque she looked.

We missed her when she went.

22

Sometimes I drove across the Alpilles to visit friends who lived in or near villages to the south of Mas des Chats. Often I returned home late. The winding road which crossed the Alpilles was, as a rule, completely deserted as I made the homeward journey, inky black under the stars or white in three-dimensional moonlight. I passed through a dream landscape, silent, eerie, so remote and lonely that I never went by without apprehension. Huge slabs of vertical rock rose high above and among the trees, pale and glowing if the moon was shining. Steep cliffs fell away beside the road and all around stood the close-knit pine forests, mile after mile of them, dark and secret, rippling with the busy night life of the wild animals of the Alpilles. Every now and then, on a curve of the south-facing road, there was a glimpse of the flood-lit fortress walls of Les Baux, rocklike themselves, floating on the sky. At the top of the hills I could see the vast, flat panorama of the plain, spreading down to the sea. Here and there were little pools of light, the glitter of street lamps among human houses. Then, on the descent to Mas des Chats, the north-facing road snaked down in darkness, only the black pines all around. Sometimes a fox stood in the beam of the headlamps, not seeming afraid, or some other small animal scurried across the road. Rarely, a rabbit, blinded by the glare of the car's lights, was pinned down in the undergrowth, paralysed with fear.

When I arrived home and opened the car door, Nero was often there to greet me. He climbed into the car at once and sat firmly on my lap. We remained in this position for a while. Nothing but night and silence, broken only by Nero's sultry purr. Getting out of the car, I brushed the row of rosemary bushes. The scent of rosemary rose into the night air and Nero bounded ahead to enter the house by the cat window.

All the cats of the household gathered slowly, rising one by one from their various resting places to join us in the kitchen. They felt it was prudent to have a little snack to prevent a serious drop in their blood sugar level before the dawn.

And Nero had his supper which he'd missed earlier in the evening,

Against the sky the cypresses made black walls and spires like churches of old cities.

because he'd been too busy stargazing, mouse hole watching, or dozing among the vines.

In the winter dusk the cats were often nervous about going out of doors for a last, quick visit. It was the time when the hungry dogs began to roam the countryside in search of food. To help them and ensure safety, I led them—each following the other—into the garden, shining my torch in the increasing dark.

In a green pearly sky the stars were coming out and in the west the orange ashes of a stunning sunset still burned.

A still, still evening, no breath of wind in the trees, anticyclonic weather, the last leaves falling singly onto already fallen leaves with a faint puttering rustle like rain. In the distance the cypresses made black walls and spires like the churches of old cities, solid black against the pellucid sky.

The cats flitted about among the bushes like small ghosts, glimpses of white, flashes of white and black. Sugar, her dark coat a camouflage, alarmingly appeared without warning, leaping wildly on to a garden seat.

After a while, I conducted the cats safely back to the house. They trooped in, one by one, obediently.

———————◇———————

As he grew older, Nero became my close companion. Grave, quiet and gentle, he was like a shadow, walking with me along the little road or between the rows of vines.

He would appear suddenly, unexpectedly from nowhere, it seemed, to be beside me. His black hair had faded to reddish brown on his broad chest. He had a sprinkle of white hairs on his underbelly. His coat gleamed. Mysterious cat, affectionate cat, like my shadow, he stayed beside me.

Sometimes, when I was tidying the kitchen, I heard a sound like rushing wings or a sudden gust of wind. Nero had flown in through the cat window. He sat composed and cool on the room divider, waiting patiently for me to offer him some food.

He had his preferred flavours in the way of tinned cat food and raw liver was his favourite dish. He was so amiable and tranquil, it was impossible to remember him as a savage brigand who had made Lily climb trees in terror and Bruno hide under tables, chattering with fear and anger.

That was long ago. Lily, although a little on edge, was prepared to share the same room with him or lie sleeping on the balcony with only a few yards between them. He was indifferent to Lily, which she realised and perhaps slightly regretted. The cat he liked was Sugar. At one point it looked as though a romance was developing between the two of them. And perhaps it might have done, given time, but Nero became ill.

He developed a chronic cystitis which returned again and again, no

As he grew older, Nero became my close companion.

matter how much treatment he had. He was already liable to very severe attacks of coughing, which might have been asthmatic in origin. These he had had as long as I'd known him. He would begin to cough suddenly, perhaps if he was purring very loudly, and the cough would increase to a crescendo, sounding as if he were suffocating. Then, the whole attack stopped. He returned to normal. Docteur Lamartin had examined him when he was under an anaesthetic for dentistry but could see nothing to cause the attacks.

That was another problem—Nero's bad teeth. His teeth were in a very decayed state, his gums infected. From time to time I took him to the clinic and the worst teeth were drawn. Then he had antibiotics for the infection of his gums. And finally, he was put onto a course of antibiotics for the infection of his bladder, which had to be prolonged indefinitely.

Nero would always show me when his bladder infection was out of control. He would come into the house and run to the litter box in Lily's room where he would try and try again—and again—unsuccessfully to pass water. His bladder was, in fact, empty and so there was no water to pass. But the infection irritated and drove him frantically to the litter box.

I learned how to help him. Quite quickly the infection could be treated. In a few hours, an injection could make him comfortable. But eventually he had to be on regular medication, given every few days or once a week.

Nero, who detested and feared all medical treatment—like most cats—was a difficult patient. But with skill and subterfuge I could give him an injection or a liquid medicine mixed in a food he liked.

Black shadow, gentle animal, I knew he'd had a hard life before he discovered the Mas des Chats. I was sad that in his old age he should have to suffer so much.

23

A cat came across the fields in the night. The fields were thick with huge weeds and tall grasses—a jungle for any cat and dangerous at night with hungry dogs roaming.

In the dawn on Sunday morning Karen and Joseph, who were staying in the little house, heard her crying outside. They were wakened for a moment, then slept again. Later she entered the Mas des Chats by the cat window, crying loudly, very aggressive and threatening. The other cats were afraid of her, cowering under tables and chairs as she flew at them.

It was easy to see that she had just given birth to kittens. It seemed her cries were meant to attract the kittens' attention, so that they would call in return and she could find them.

She cried loudly, short painful cries with hardly a pause. While she cried, she searched. She went all over the house. She looked in cupboards and on shelves. She searched every corner.

She must have lost the kittens immediately or soon after they were born. Perhaps a fox or starving dog had killed them. Perhaps a human being had taken them and destroyed them while she had briefly left them.

In the afternoon I made my usual round of the neighbourhood, asking if anyone knew anything of her. As usual the answer was no. She might have come for miles across the fields, driven to search for her young. Her coat was full of grass seeds and burrs and she was starving, although not very thin.

Karen and Joseph took her to the little house to feed her, away from the other cats. When Karen picked her up, she felt her as a light, formless heap, her muscles rubbery, her limbs without tension. We thought she was very tired and perhaps had a fever, following the birth. But she ate ravenously.

Her colouring was particularly beautiful. Her coat was soft, ashy grey and black with a dapple of pale pink, and her face was sooty. Her eyes were round and golden, sad, angry eyes.

Karen and Joseph were at once enchanted by her. She quickly

became affectionate—someone's pet, a tame cat now hopelessly lost.

Her crying went on and on and she was restless, not well, I thought.

Next day they took her to the vet. Docteur Arbois was not sure what was wrong. She had certainly just given birth to kittens and she did have a fever. She also had some swollen glands. Her muscles were toneless and limp. He suggested we should wait a few days, giving her treatment to recover from the effects of the pregnancy. We should take her temperature every day and she should be kept away from the other cats. He would see her again at the end of the week. If she was no better he would take some blood and test for cat leukaemia.

Quite quickly, she settled down. The pills helped her to recover from the loss of the kittens and she no longer cried.

Karen and Joseph enjoyed looking after her. The pathos of her made them spoil her and all three were happy. She was fed on delicious meals; she was given toys to play with; they brushed her coat. They gave her a name—Marie. She relaxed and bloomed. But she refused to leave the house. Often, she lay limp and tired on her bed and seemed unable to jump onto chairs or sofa. The fever, although slight, continued. But she ate well and responded charmingly to the cherishing of Karen and Joseph.

At the end of the week Docteur Calan, another member of the team of vets at the clinic, came to see Nero who was very ill, and Billy the dog. He looked at Marie and took some blood for the test for *leucose*, cat leukaemia.

'Why,' I asked him, 'are there so many cats—tame and domesticated which obviously once had a home, gentle and affectionate cats—roaming around here, lost or abandoned . . . ?'

He said, 'Here in the country, and in the town, there are lots of people who rent houses and apartments. They live in the house for a year or two and while they're there they have a cat—they find one, or a friend's cat has kittens and they take one . . . Then they move away, leave the house and the cat. Perhaps they think the next tenants will look after the cat—but sometimes it's a month or two or longer before the house is occupied again, and the next tenants may not want the cat. The cats wander off—try to find food—get ill . . .'

He gave a sad shrug, smiled and drove away, saying that we should

The pathos of Marie made them spoil her. She ate well and responded charmingly to their cherishing.

have the result of the blood test in the morning.

We were nervous and anxious, dreading a positive result. If she were found to be suffering from that terrible illness, incurable and infectious, we should have to have her life ended. Karen, who felt deeply protective towards all small and helpless creatures, had already invested much love in this little cat—more than love, a profound identification with her plight. Joseph, too, was full of tenderness for her.

I was apprehensive for all three.

In the morning, the test was positive.

Docteur Calan spoke gently and sensibly to me. One might be able to keep Marie alive for a little longer with large doses of antibiotics and steroids—but she already had a fever and swollen glands. Inevitably, quite soon other more cruel and painful symptoms would appear. He would advise that her life be ended now.

I agreed, but discussed the possibilities first with Karen and Joseph. We decided Docteur Calan was right.

In the afternoon, the two went out to visit friends. I remained at home because I thought it best this way—to deal with the dreaded visit of the vet.

I led him to the little house.

Eagerly, trustingly, Marie ran towards me—always to be remembered as trusting and eager and happy to see me—then suddenly taken aback as I lifted her and the needle with the tranquilliser went into her skin. Then the lethal liquid and, very quickly, without pain or understanding, she was dead.

I was left with her little body. Her coat now seemed ragged, a heap of soft uneven fur, infinitely pathetic.

I buried her in a grave which Joseph had prepared on the edge of the vineyard.

The sky was full of swallows flying southward, flying to the warm south, circling and eddying and drifting as they went, but moving always south. I stood on the edge of the vineyard by Marie's grave and felt alone, isolated, left behind, wretched.

Poor little cat who had the cards stacked against her, symbol of all who are out of luck and beyond help, the cards stacked against them too . . . Sadly, I went back into the little house. I cleaned and tidied so as to leave no trace of Marie. I took the litter tray, the toys, the half-eaten saucer of food. I tried to remove all reminders of the pretty little cat which would hurt Karen and Joseph. I didn't know that there was a half-full tin of Whiskas in the fridge, which they solemnly handed to me the following day. Otherwise, I left the place as if Marie had never been.

Next day, I asked Monsieur Mercier to put a large stone on Marie's grave so that the roaming dogs would not dig up the body. Later, I saw that Karen had carefully placed a small plastic jar with pink flowers in it on top of the stone.

The wind knocked it over, scattering the flowers.

24

However rough and gruff Monsieur le Gris was with her, Baby continued to be infatuated by him. Watching her gentle, persistent and finally successful attempts to persuade him to caress her, I remembered how I had rescued her from the fields one day by using him as a lure.

She had been ill for a few days, not eating, but looking sleepy and ruffled. She was wild at that time and not ill enough to collapse indoors, as had happened with her attack of cat 'flu.

Instead she went to the garden or fields to hide. I searched for her. I found her tucked under a huge tangle of briars where I couldn't reach her. Later I went to look for her again in the hopes of getting her indoors. She had moved from the briars and was nowhere to be seen.

I went through the vineyard and the neighbouring fields calling. She didn't respond. So I decided to try to lure her home with the help of Monsieur le Gris.

To his astonishment and indignation I picked him up briskly from his comfortable bed in the dining-room and carried him, staggering slightly with the weight of him, to the road beside the vineyard. He was too surprised to struggle and by the time he had pulled himself together sufficiently to make a strong protest, we were already some way up the road.

I put him down. While he was repairing the damage I'd done to his immaculately groomed coat, I called Baby again.

Miraculously, she appeared. She came out of the thick undergrowth at the edge of the Corbets' field looking sleepy and tired but happy to see her dear le Gris.

I then had to persuade him to return home. He was all for having a bit of a walk round the field. Baby walked beside him, and when Monsieur le Gris felt it was time for supper, Baby came along as well. They both went into the kitchen together after which, mercifully, she remained indoors.

And next morning, she was much better.

25

One winter, my neighbour Monsieur Corbet died suddenly. The way in which he died was sad—tragic—but had a comic side. He himself would have laughed. When he was in good spirits he laughed easily, often at himself. Even when he was depressed, as he had been in the last months of his life, he could laugh a little, at least when he was talking to me.

When he died he was lying in the chaise longue in a corner of their kitchen. It had been put there so that he could rest without having to go to their bedroom upstairs.

He had eaten an excellent lunch. Madame Corbet had prepared his favourite courgettes with tomato, followed by a small steak, lightly grilled, with baked potatoes, and then a piece of good camembert. After they had finished the meal, he lay on the chaise longue, about to have a snooze. He was eating a piece of nougat and, smiling, held out the box to his wife to offer her one, gave a deep groan and died.

For him, this way of death was merciful, as Madame Corbet agreed, in spite of the terrible loss. He had dreaded illness and the business of dying.

All his life he had worked on the land, the child of generations of farmers, *paysans*. When the war came in 1939 he was immediately conscripted into the French infantry, then was taken prisoner by the Germans within a month or two of military service. He was sent to work on the land on a farm near the cold Polish border of Germany.

He spent the next six years as a prisoner of war—six of the most important years in a young man's life. He used to talk about it fragmentarily.

'*En Écosse*, whisky . . .' he would say, smiling broadly. It was to Scotland that his regiment was sent before taking ship for France. Then a few German words, mostly about food: '*Kartoffel, Brot, Guten Tag, Wurst* . . .'

The farm people where he worked never talked directly to him, being forbidden to fraternise. But they let him share their midday meal. He sat at the table—or nearby—ate and listened. At night, he went back to the prison camp. Being shy, he made no friends among the other prisoners. So passed six long years.

When the war ended he was brought back to Provence. He began to work his land which he had inherited from his father. After a while he married, and on Armistice Day each year he marched proudly in the town together with the other *anciens combattants de guerre*, bearing the *Tricolor*. A small band played and the Mayor gave a speech. Monsieur Corbet wore his beret pulled well down and his medals on his chest.

I once asked Madame Corbet what life was like under the German occupation of France. Madame Corbet's face became impassive, mask-like. It was only after knowing her for some time that I understood that when her face became frozen, her eyes unseeing, she wasn't trying to hide her feelings from the eyes of others but concealing them from herself, shielding herself from the pain of them. She was noncommittal about the Germans in Provence and I learned nothing from her.

I knew nothing, either, about how she met her husband—whether they fell in love, or whether it was an arranged marriage. He was stunted by all those years as a prisoner of war. She was strong, plain, honest, direct and marvellously loyal and dutiful. The marriage seems to have worked well, but it was a sorrow to her to have had no children. Sharing delicious food was a huge common interest.

She cooked, he liked to know what was going on in the kitchen and to help, taste and advise.

'*Elle est très bonne, la soupe au Pistou,*' he would shout at me—shout because of his extreme deafness . . . or, nodding and half-shutting his eyes . . . '*Goutez . . . Goutez . . .*' as I was presented with a little dish of ratatouille—or olives which they had cured themselves or mushrooms picked in the woods.

Madame Corbet would sometimes bring round a jar of soup still hot, or aubergine, lightly fried, or orange liqueur, home-made.

At Christmas, he gathered wild holly which was made up into bunches to give to relations and friends. I was always very pleased to have mine. At the right seasons they picked wild asparagus and the mushrooms which pushed up under the cypress hedges after rain, always in the same place.

He was a countryman in his blood and bones, deeply bound in the earth and the tilling of it and the growing of fruits and vegetables.

But in addition, he had a huge general knowledge acquired through reading and watching the television. He knew everything that was going on in the world beyond Provence.

'Your *Dame de Fer* (as the French invariably called Mrs Thatcher) made a good speech last night,' or, 'A pity the ground nuts scheme for Africa was such a failure . . .'

He was interested in the stars and the forests of the Amazon—and the British Royal Family, like everyone else in France.

Once he had a glimpse of the Queen and the Duke of Edinburgh. He joined the crowd lining the road as the Royal Family drove to lunch at a famous restaurant in Les Baux. He loved to talk about this incident. I heard the story again and again. 'Prince Charles was in the back of the car,' he'd tell me, leaving the 's' off Charles' name.

The main theme of his life, the basis of it, was the growing of French beans, his treasure, his gold. He had a dog called Dick, whom he dearly loved, and the family cat, Frisquette. The cat was supposed to belong to Madame Corbet, but I think it was he who mainly cared about it. He made Dick do circus tricks for the reward of salted peanuts and cocktail biscuits. Dick obliged, awkwardly. Frisquette he would hold by the nape of her neck and, as she dangled, shake her—not very hard. She cringed.

Both these sights disturbed me. I was aware of a raw, unknowing cruelty in Monsieur Corbet and also in his wife. But a great ability to love was in them too.

About eight months before he died, the Corbets gave up their work in the fields. Monsieur Corbet was made by his wife to retire. No more vegetables, no more beans—except for a small patch near the house. She was tired—understandably. Her back needed resting. He wouldn't be able to manage alone and paid help was out of the question. Her back ached. Her arms ached. She had planted and sown and watered and weeded and sprayed and picked French beans and other vegetables for almost half her life. She was growing old—and he was well into his seventies.

But Monsieur Corbet was not suited to retirement. As soon as he had

About eight months before he died, Monsieur Corbet was made by his wife to retire. No more vegetables, no more beans—except for a small patch near the house.

no work to do, he fell into depression. He took the dog Dick on walks in the neighbouring fields. Dick, at first, tugged him along at the end of the short heavy chain. My sister, Nora, visiting during the summer, gave them an extensible lead. This was an improvement for Dick, but Monsieur Corbet looked hunched and dreary, the beret he always wore pulled well down on his brow, his eyes sad, his face twisted in utter boredom.

Then, suddenly, Dick was ill. Within days, he died of cancer, the vet said—a terrible loss.

After this Monsieur Corbet would not or could not eat or sleep. The doctor prescribed anti-depressant pills, sedatives, sleeping pills.

Madame Corbet suffered almost as much as he did. Lines of stress appeared in her face, already worn by years in blazing sun and fierce wind. She cooked the most tempting and delicious meals which Monsieur Corbet wouldn't touch.

He was silent, or irritable or angry, and he became terrified of illness, terrified of dying.

He had suffered some years earlier a coronary thrombosis. But he had survived that well and lived a normal farmer's life doing heavy, physical work. He saw his doctor regularly and he told me, every now and then, what his blood pressure was or his serum cholesterol.

The day he died he had seen the doctor in the morning and had been told he was in excellent condition. This news had cheered him very much and he had come home with a good appetite. So his last day was a happy one. He ate and enjoyed the lunch, took a piece of nougat, and died.

I heard the news in the afternoon. Madame Corbet's sister telephoned. I went over to her *mas* to find a solemn collection of women gathered around Madame Corbet, who was wearing her impassive face.

A funeral service followed a lying in state. In due course, Monsieur Corbet's body was buried in the Corbet family tomb.

Madame Corbet kept strict mourning for a year, wearing only black. She visited her husband's grave almost daily, refreshing the flowers, removing dead plants. The following year she wore black with white or mauve. She still visited the grave very often and made sure the flowers were in good order.

To honour her husband's memory, she arranged that the fields around their *mas* be kept tidy, turned over by a tractor twice a year, because that was what he would have wanted. Meanwhile she looked for a town house, either an old one or something more modern—a 'veella' as she called it.

She had never learned to drive, but rode her *mobylette*, a Vespa-like machine, like a Valkyrie.

Eventually, after inspecting and rejecting a great many houses, she found her 'villa', a plain bungalow set among other bungalows in a quiet corner not far from the Roman antiquities. It was a pleasant house, light, comfortable, well built, an easy walk from the town centre. She had bought it for her old age, she told me. She would never move again.

The villa had a quiet little garden looking south and a pink bathroom which she loved.

I visited her. She showed me round. There was a smell of polish and cleanness. Fresh lace curtains covered the windows. Red geraniums flourished on the terrace. I told her I admired the place and how well she had arranged her sparse furniture. She was pleased—but added sadly, 'If only Gaston could be here with me, it would be a *veritable paradis.*'

I silently believed that Gaston would have found it hellish to be so confined. He loved the fields and the great sky and the cypress hedges and the hills. And yet, perhaps he might have adjusted—taken little walks in the town, pottered out to watch the men playing *boules* in the nearby square, mown the grass . . .

Before she moved to the town, Madame Corbet's cat, Frisquette, died—or rather, had to be helped to die. She had become ill, and after a few visits to the vet it was clear nothing could be done to save her. She was suffering, in pain, it seemed.

I drove Madame Corbet and Frisquette to the vet, Frisquette confined to a basket, for the final injection. On the way, Madame Corbet was talking animatedly when Frisquette let out a long, despairing, heart-rending howl.

'*Tais toi*, Frisquette!'

Madame Corbet's forceful shout silenced the poor cat until we arrived at the vet, when Frisquette howled again—and again. Madame Corbet shouted, '*Tais toi*, Frisquette!' without the faintest affection or sympathy. And she refused to accompany Frisquette into the room where she was to die, to my deep dismay.

Docteur Lamartin said to me soothingly, 'There exist people who don't want to see . . .' and he promised to deal with Frisquette immediately.

Perhaps Madame Corbet's hardness was like her impassive expression—a way of keeping her feelings under control.

So Madame Corbet moved to the town without dog or cat and she refused to take another animal.

117

Her life became quite jolly in a way that was never possible when her husband was alive. All her relations rallied round her and helped her put and keep her place in order. I admired her for her determination and courage.

There was another trait in her which astonished me—and which I also admired. She continued to prepare and eat food for herself, with just the same care and elaborateness as when she lived with Gaston. She showed me one day what she intended to eat for lunch—a very pretty vegetable salad, beautifully arranged in a little glass dish, finely sliced beef in a mushroom sauce, *pommes dauphinois* . . . and a few raspberries.

She also gave lunch and dinner parties for her relations. Sometimes as many as twelve people sat round her table. Her husband could never have accepted such entertaining.

She missed and mourned him all the same. Several times I went with her to the cemetery. I watched her heave large pots of flowers into position, water plants, trim dead leaves and stems, stand back and stare at the tomb where he lay.

I also stared, seeing him as I'd known him, a square, solid man with powerful shoulders and short legs, beret pulled down over a large brow, kind, rugged features, a radiant smile; a generous man, easily angered, passionately in love with the land. I tried to see him as a young man, shouted at by Nazi troops, hustled into a train that took him on a long, long journey to six hot summers and six bitter winters, confused, bewildered, imprisoned among foreign people speaking a language he couldn't understand . . . straining to understand . . . dreaming of Provence.

Did anyone write to him—censored letters . . . send him food parcels, cigarettes . . .? And if so, what did the letters say, what could they say over six years of war as he wondered, would he ever get back—ever see Provence again?

26

Oedipus once came back from his journeys ill. He refused to eat, lay limp and weary on a sofa in the salon. He must have had a high fever but it was impossible to take his temperature.

I asked Docteur Lamartin to visit him. He came, and while I did my best to hold the struggling Oedipus, pushed a needle in his flank, giving him a long-acting, slow-release antibiotic.

'He has pneumonia,' he said to me.

'How do you know?'

'When a *matou* comes home ill in this weather, he has pneumonia. It is normal.'

Docteur Lamartin smiled and was about to leave, then stopped a moment to make a note for the computer which registered all patients at the clinic.

'What is his name?'

'Oedipus—or rather Oedipe . . .'

'No, no, Oedipus, Oedipussy—I understand . . .'

He left—and Oedipussy recovered.

There were times when the cats and dogs seemed to be endlessly ill, one after another—with toothache or earache or pneumonia or infected bites. I became quite despairing and desperate, visiting the veterinary clinic almost every other day, fetching medicines or ferrying animals to and fro. At the clinic they were helpful and supportive.

'It's the time of the year,' said Madame Grasse, the marvellously efficient receptionist who gave good advice and reassurance to animal owners all day long, with quiet patience. 'When the weather changes things will improve.

'With so many animals,' she would tell me, 'there's bound to be one who gets ill every now and then.'

Docteur Lamartin handled his clients and their pets with exquisite tact and great expertise. He understood only too well the emotions that people invest in their animals, and he respected feelings.

'Cats are difficult,' he would say sympathetically, 'especially ones that have been rescued from the wild. Dogs are easier!' and he smiled

There were times when the cats seemed to be endlessly ill, but on this occasion Oedipus recovered.

on Caramel—who always enjoyed a visit to the clinic—and gave her a pat.

'*Les chats sont difficiles*' was something I often heard.

When I was buying cat food at the supermarket, the girl at the cash desk, counting my tins, enquired, '*Est-ce que vos chats sont difficiles?*'

'Very,' I replied. 'Do you have a cat?'

'Yes, when I lived at home. Now, no. My mother has fifteen cats.'

'Are they difficult?'

'Yes.' She smiled timidly.

'All cats are difficult,' I said, and she agreed, a little sadly.

27

Grisette was a gypsy, a pretty vagabond.

Madame Corbet came over one day to see if the wild asparagus plants at the feet of the cypresses had yet produced any edible stems. It was before she moved to her bungalow in the town. In the course of conversation she said a kitten had appeared on her doorstep the day before, a beautiful little kitten with a tiny red collar. The collar was embroidered with pearls.

'Then he—or she—must have belonged to someone?'

'She must. But to whom? She's so small, this kitten, it's hard to imagine she came from very far away . . .'

'Are you feeding her? Is she old enough to eat?'

'Yes, she can eat.'

Madame Corbet was noncommittal on the matter of feeding the kitten. She didn't want to admit to feeding it herself. The Moroccans next door, the children seemed to be feeding it, she thought, when Maurice was fed . . .

Maurice, my Moroccan neighbours' cat, ate largely at my house. I suspected that Madame Corbet gave the kitten a little of this or that from her own meals, but didn't want to take official responsibility for its welfare.

When next I saw her, I asked, 'How's the kitten?' By now its sex was determined—a female—and she had a name, Grisette.

Madame Corbet, I could see, was growing fond of her.

'Is she still wearing the red collar with the pearls?'

She was, but she was growing bigger and the collar was tiny. It might have to come off soon. After a moment, she said she thought Grisette must have belonged to a child.

'Why?'

'Such a pretty little kitten and such a pretty little collar . . .'

The next time we talked of Grisette, it seemed she was pregnant. Maurice, it was thought, was responsible.

And when we talked again, Grisette, although very young, had given birth to three fine kittens in Madame Corbet's garage. Madame Corbet seemed very pleased. The kittens were doing well.

There followed a tragic mishap.

'We shouldn't have done it,' Madame Corbet said again and again. 'We shouldn't have touched them, I know. But we were just looking at them and Malika was saying which one did I like and which one she liked and we picked them up to look at them better . . .'

She looked deeply troubled but tried to smile. 'Well, then Grisette was very upset. She's taken them away—somewhere—I don't know where, I've looked but I can't find them and she's gone—she's disappeared . . .'

Madame Corbet had searched and searched. She could find no trace of the kittens, she couldn't hear them crying. And Grisette had vanished. Madame Corbet looked—and felt—distressed and guilty, but there was nothing to be done.

In the evening of the same day, I saw a small, strange cat prowling among the bushes by the terrace, a light greyish-blonde cat with, I thought, a red collar, but about that I wasn't sure. The cat ran off as I came near.

And returned, appearing for a moment in the cat window, then darting away again. This time, I clearly saw a narrow red collar with a slight glitter which must have been the pearls. It was Grisette. I telephoned Madame Corbet to tell her the news.

No sign of the kittens, however. She had, it turned out later, abandoned them, after removing them, one by one, from Madame Corbet's garage.

Grisette then appeared more often at the Mas des Chats, attracted by food and the presence of the other cats. She tripped in through the cat window at meal-times, was given a dish of food, ate timidly and fast and hurried away.

By now, she was a very charming-looking young cat, light in colour with large, slanting blue-grey-green eyes. A narrow line of ash grey ran from the outer point of her eyes to her ears, giving her a made-up, slightly artificial look.

Of the kittens no more was seen or heard, but Grisette herself, soon afterwards, installed herself as a cat of the household, largely encouraged by Monsieur le Gris. With him, it was love at first sight. He was

Grisette was a charming-looking young cat. She installed herself as a cat of the household, largely encouraged by Monsieur le Gris.

enchanted by Grisette—and she happily accepted his endearments and caresses.

She refused absolutely to return to Madame Corbet's house or to the Moroccans. When carried over there, she ran away, fast, as soon as she was put down.

Madame Corbet's and Malika's handling of her kittens must have disturbed her deeply. She was not altogether tame, but she allowed me to stroke her while remaining a little distant, a little reserved. Soon, it was necessary to have her sterilised. There was no room for any more kittens at Mas des Chats. The operation went smoothly and Grisette recovered quickly.

Monsieur le Gris continued to adore her. He would lick her and play with her anywhere at any time of the day or night. She grew larger, more and more handsome. The little red collar with the pearls constricted her neck.

I removed it, kept it sentimentally—have it still: a very small, bright red collar with an elaborate design of miniature pearls, glittering.

Then Grisette became restless. I now think I should have accustomed her to a place of her own, a room at the *mas* which she could look on as hers, her space—as I did for Sugar and other newcomers. I should have shut her in for a week or so and fed her there and made a fuss of her—and put butter on her paws. She might then have developed a sense of belonging to the place.

As it was, I let her wander.

She began to go off—in a way unusual for female cats especially when sterilised—on long excursions. She was sometimes away for hours. Sometimes she left in the morning and was away until midnight or later.

I waited for her. I fed her when she came back, however late it was. She looked worried. She looked distressed. She was unhappy and unsettled. She became wilder.

I was anxious for her.

Where did she go? It must have been a long way away. Sometimes, when she returned, she was hardly hungry. Had she found another home where she was fed? Or had she been hunting and eaten mice or birds?

Waiting for her to come back at night I used to go out into the dark or the moonlit garden. Sometimes I saw her returning briskly over the little bridge leading down from the *colline*. But I didn't always see her return and perhaps at times she crossed the fields. I discussed her journeys with Madame Corbet.

She was a little bitter about Grisette. She said: 'Grisette left one home to come to me. Then she left me to go to you. Now she's left you. Grisette's a wanderer, a gypsy. It's her nature.'

Grisette came home later and later every night. But she did come back. Then one night she didn't appear and I never saw her again.

The night she vanished was brightly lit. A huge silver moon shone in the winter sky. About midnight, looking out of an upstairs window in the hope of seeing Grisette, I saw instead a large fox on the terrace— exceptionally large. He moved about, grunting. After a while he went off, over the fields, but he might have been up on the hill before he arrived at Mas des Chats.

Was he perhaps responsible for Grisette's death?

Foxes, they say, don't normally attack cats, but it was a very cold, frosty night—icy—and the fox might have been very hungry. Grisette, I thought, was careless on her journeys and might have been taken unaware.

Perhaps it was just a coincidence—and yet . . . I did a tour of the neighbourhood.

On the other side of the *colline* there was the house of an absent American woman who had a French gardener-*gardien*, a pleasant, friendly young man. I visited him. I described Grisette. Yes, he knew her. She came often through the garden—almost every day. But he hadn't seen her since the night she didn't return home to me. He was quite clear and certain.

Some other accident could have befallen Grisette. A car might have hit her. She might have been shot or poisoned. The hunters were around in winter.

I asked elsewhere. I asked everywhere, every house in the neighbourhood. No one knew anything of her.

A farmer nearby who owned many greenhouses said: 'A female cat? They don't go far from home. She should return . . . unless something happened to her . . .'

Did she find another home? I think she would have returned to the Mas des Chats from time to time.

I miss her. I mourn for her.

Her little red collar with the pearls still lies, as such objects tend to do, in a pot in the kitchen which also contains rubber bands, the stopper of a bottle, some screws and a small screw-driver.

28

Maurice, the one-eyed cat who belonged to the Moroccan-Spanish family next door, used to visit Mas des Chats regularly for food. Ill-treated himself, he was bad-tempered and often savage with the other cats. He leapt through the cat window snarling and cursing. The household cats were afraid of him and trod warily away when he was in his worst moods. With me, he was affectionate. He rubbed against my legs with a deep, growling purr. He ate ravenously, as if he were never fed at home. If it hadn't been for his one-eyed clownish look, he would have been a beautiful cat. His tabby coat was finely marked, with broad ribbons of symmetrical black against pale grey fur.

I noticed one day that he was becoming thinner—and he slowly became increasingly thin. His back-bone was visible through his skin. His muscles wasted. He began to eat less. Maurice was ill. He came over and stared at his dish of food, picked at it and went away. Then he didn't eat at all.

I hesitated about going over to talk to his owners. The last time I had been to see Malika, to discuss Maurice's infected eye, she had been insulting and hostile. She knew how to treat Maurice. She would bathe the eye. I offered, tactfully, to take care of the vet's fee. She waved me away, her strong face—half-African, half-Arab—mocking. Maurice *had* to go to the vet, in the end, as an emergency, and the eye had to be removed. I knew I would have no better reaction from her now.

I happened, then, to meet Malika at the supermarket. In the course of conversation I said, 'What has happened to Maurice? He's ill, I think.' Malika looked quite taken aback, genuinely astonished. I could see she hadn't even noticed Maurice's condition.

I said, 'He used to come over every day—visiting my cats, you know. Now I haven't seen him for days . . .'

Malika collected her wits and a ready answer rose to her lips.

'Oh, Maurice is all right—he's fine. My niece is here staying with us. She loves him—when she's here he doesn't leave the place—she plays with him all the time . . .'

I asked Madame Corbet, 'Have you seen Maurice?'

She couldn't really remember whether she had or not.

Some weeks later, I saw Malika again when I was visiting Madame Corbet.

'Any news of Maurice?' I asked.

She looked a bit sheepish.

'No.' She laughed slightly. 'It's funny. He seems to have disappeared,' and she added that ever-useful blanket phrase used by all the uncaring animal owners in the district when talking about pets which had vanished, for whatever reason: 'He must have been *ecrasé sur la route*—run over.'

But I knew perfectly well that Maurice had taken his suffering and emaciated little body into the fields and there, alone, he had died.

29

He was small and stocky, cheerful, good-natured, brave and a bit of a rogue like everyone else.

I knew him as a laughing man, of immense energy, devoted to his family and a loving father to his two sons. He was the postman but also an *agriculteur*, a tiller of the earth, a grower of vegetables and fruit, being born into a family of farmers. He looked after the vines in my vineyard, doing the work in return for the grapes. These he could sell for a good profit if the weather was favourable and if he had taken proper care of the vines.

His heart gave trouble. Years before he had had severe coronary disease. The doctors had performed an operation to give his heart an additional blood supply, a by-pass of the blocked arteries.

This procedure worked well for a time, but after I had been at Mas des Chats for a few years, his heart gave trouble again. He was put on sick leave. Meanwhile, temporary postmen and women, who couldn't always find my house, delivered the letters.

Sometimes he looked after the vines properly. Some years his other occupations and interests took priority. His artichokes, his olives, his hens, his melons, his strawberries, his son's move to Lyon, his holiday at the seaside, his apricots, his cherries, and the birth of a grandchild prevented him giving the vines the treatment they needed. Then the grapes would suffer, be diseased or shrunken or dry.

During the fifth year of my living at Mas des Chats he was particularly neglectful. I threatened, as I had done many times before, to find someone else to look after the vineyard—or to have the vines pulled up. As always he was apologetic and reassuring. He laughed, ruefully, his blue eyes laughing too. He understood. I was right. Next year he'd do better.

And in the sixth year he actually did turn over the earth, spray, fertilise and prune as he should have done. He even planted new vines where the old ones had died and added two rows of them to the farther vineyard.

The result was a bumper crop of grapes.

The harvest was, as always, a noisy, happy, family occasion. His

The postman was a laughing man, of immense energy. He looked after the vines in my vineyard.

wife, as short as he was and completely square and solid, was there, dressed in a thick red woollen sweater and tight red trousers. His mother-in-law, the same shape as his wife, wore a grey cardigan and a modest skirt. His two sons were there with their girlfriends or wives and there was a sister-in-law, I think, or sister of Madame Sabin.

All worked hard (except perhaps the girlfriends), shouting to one another, laughing, snipping, gossiping. Basket after basket of grapes was loaded in the van.

I went out to talk to them.

The week before there had been storms which luckily didn't spoil the grapes. More bad weather was forecast, but, on the day of the *vendange*, there was bright sunshine and a brisk, fresh wind.

'Just as well not to wait till next week,' I said to the postman.

He laughed.

'Next week I'll be in Marseille,' he said, 'in hospital.'

'What! Why?'

He tapped his chest.

'They tell me I have to have another operation.'

'Oh no!' I was dismayed.

'The arteries—they're in very bad shape, they're going to do another by-pass. *Five* new arteries this time.'

'But you look so well!'

'I *am* well. I can do the work . . .' he gestured around us, 'but they say it's absolutely necessary. They did the test—they could see everything blocked up, they said. And yet—I don't have any pain . . .'

I wanted very much to say, 'Don't go, Monsieur Sabin. Put it off. Don't go!' I said nothing.

He laughed again.

'I'm afraid,' he said. 'I'm afraid I might die.'

'Oh no!' I said. 'No, of course you won't die.' But I also was afraid.

In the week that followed, a friend telephoned.

'Did you hear?' she said. 'Monsieur Sabin is dead.'

Later I learned he had died following the operation. There were complications, a haemorrhage. They had had to open up his chest again. He was eighteen hours under the anaesthetic. His heart stopped. In spite of every effort to get it going, it would not beat again.

131

30

I saw that Hélène was muttering something unflattering, if not actually insulting, to Curly Thomas as she passed him on the room divider in the kitchen on her way upstairs. Her nerves were in any case on edge and she was in a bitter mood, having had to endure being shut up in her room for half-an-hour or so in the late afternoon.

Curly Thomas, dozing with his eyes half-shut, looking like an old monkey or an ancient Chinese philosopher, replied to her, I thought, in the vein of 'Sticks and stones may break my bones but words . . .' and Hélène sped away and raced up the stairs. The old cat was called Curly Thomas for two reasons.

'Curly' because his ears (in any case tiny, for hereditary reasons, I imagine) had been bitten in innumerable fights into two small wavy structures, stuck closely to his head. He looked almost earless. That, linked to the fact that he had a pair of wonderful large and lucent eyes, gave him his monkey look.

'Thomas' was added to 'Curly' by Karen who felt that 'Curly' was too flippant a name for such a sad and dignified old fellow. I had called him Curly for years. He had been coming for food almost as long as I had lived in the *mas*. Years before he had been a strong, aggressive animal whom the other cats had feared. Now they laughed at him or despised him, thinking him an old fool, and they might be offensive to him as Hélène had been. Monsieur le Gris had been known to snarl and jump at him at times. I liked him and knew he was anything but a fool.

Curly was never supposed to be a cat of the household, and until his first illness he was an 'outside' cat who came only to eat, then went away. His two extreme illnesses—one following quickly on the other—turned him into a resident member of the household.

With his first illness he became emaciated and wouldn't or couldn't eat. It was summer and he didn't come indoors. He lay around on the terrace outside the little house, looking so gaunt and exhausted it was thought he would soon die. He had wounds on his head, a triangle of deep bites which looked as though they went through his skull right into his brain. I asked the vet for advice and he gave me some powerful antibiotic injections mixed with cortisone.

I was able to give him three of these daily injections because he lay for hours, hardly moving, on a small garden table on the terrace, in front of the little house. He seemed almost unconscious and didn't notice the needle passing into his skin.

Then he disappeared. We all thought he must have gone away to die.

But after a few days he returned and began to eat a little, then was hungry for more. Skeletal still, he was miraculously saved from death.

Only a few weeks later he was desperately ill again.

This time he had coryza or cat 'flu in a severe form. I shut him up in the salon and asked the vet to call.

Antibiotics again in heavy doses—a variety of them was required—and once again that tough old cat survived. It took a long time for him to recover completely and he was only skin and bone. But he lived.

I swear he was grateful to me. In his mysterious cat way he seemed to acknowledge that I'd cared for him, gruffly expressing his thanks.

Then he began to eat. He ate and ate and drank milk in huge quantities, all day long, day after day. Slowly he regained weight and strength. Now he remained at Mas des Chats, choosing a place on the kitchen room divider to call his own. Karen loved him. She saw in him the debilitated, the weak pushed to the wall, the underprivileged, the disadvantaged. He was all of those things. He was also noble and courageous. So to give him dignity, she added Thomas to his name.

I discovered as time went by that he had many endearing characteristics—and some less endearing ones. On the negative side he was a thief, stealing food wherever his very skilled nose told him he'd find it. He jumped up on to kitchen tables and into cupboards if the doors were left ajar. No dish could be left uncovered or unattended without his finding it and helping himself to a little meal. This must have been an old habit of his which helped him keep going in times when his food supply was meagre. He wasn't prepared to give it up even though, at Mas des Chats, he was given as much food as he could eat.

In addition, he let out a wild, loud wail, repeated again and again, when he was demanding food—which he would do relentlessly, even though his stomach and his dish were full.

In his mysterious cat way, Curly Thomas seemed to acknowledge that I'd cared for him.

And his third misdemeanour was to leave little traces of urine here and there in the house to testify to his ownership of it.

On the positive side he was an intelligent, very affectionate cat. He had a childlike quality of innocence and candour. He particularly liked to go upstairs and fold himself into a little basket which had once been used as a sewing basket.

When Monsieur le Gris attacked Curly Thomas in the kitchen—and Monsieur le Gris couldn't abide him—he would shrink back and hang his head meekly and sheepishly. Sometimes le Gris, not content with snarling and growling and pushing him about, went so far as to slap the poor old creature. Curly Thomas would retreat, in a sad, beaten way, behind a piece of furniture and stare with large, unhappy eyes at the angry, robust figure of stout le Gris. Yet in other circumstances Curly was a fearless fighter, as his torn ears and wounded head testified. He was ferocious with the visiting outside cats whom, given his way, he would never have allowed to eat in the house. He loved me to stroke his ragged head. He purred loudly and sidled backwards and forwards. When he didn't go up to the little basket, he continued to use as his bed a small square of towel on the kitchen room divider—accepting a second class citizen status. He lay curled up in this little space looking, I thought, like an untouchable sleeping on a pavement mat in Bombay.

I tried to help him be well and strong by feeding him heartily—and his appetite, when he was fit, was enormous.

31

Almost every day, at some moment or another, the garden at Mas des Chats echoed with the sound of an ugly, raucous shriek. This was Emilie's cry, the outcome of an encounter with her enemy, Monsieur le Gris.

Monsieur le Gris hated Emilie. He had done so from the moment he first sighted her, years before, when Hélène had brought her children, Oedipus and Emilie, down from the *colline* to establish them at Mas des Chats.

The kittens had been born in a deep hollow just above the little bridge which spanned the stream. Hélène had chosen this place after discovering the cat bowl, put out each evening at the back of the house. Once she realised she had a regular supply of food she must have searched for a safe refuge to rear her young. The hollow had steep, rough sides covered in thick brambles. She could protect them among the thorns and tangle of stems. They spent their first weeks under sun and stars.

I used to visit them.

I watched them grow—two little wild cats of the *garrigue*.

When they were old enough, Hélène brought them down to eat with her at the cat bowl. Then, at a time which she judged suitable, she announced she was preparing to establish herself and her children at the *mas*.

She took no notice of my protests. She and her children entered the house—difficult for little creatures who had had no contact at all with humans.

Oedipus, bolder and stronger than his sister, became in the end a cat of the household. He was helped by Monsieur le Gris who loved him as much as he hated Emilie.

Emilie followed her instincts and remained wild. She left the house. I tried to feed and protect her. She became a vagrant. She came and went, a flicker of white cat, now here, now gone, appearing out of nowhere and, after eating the food put down for her in her chosen place, disappearing with a toss of her head and a flick of her tail.

Emilie had no territory, no resting place of her own. She was restless, a roving refugee, a *sans abri*.

My sister Nora called her the ghost—so ephemeral was that small white shape, so mysterious were its comings and goings. She was quite wild, but she depended on me for food and she would often—not always—turn up to eat once or twice in twenty-four hours.

She had a hard time surviving. Monsieur le Gris hounded her mercilessly and the other cats followed his example. She had no territory, no resting place of her own. She was restless, a roving refugee, a *sans abri*.

Emilie was given her name in memory of a sad child who at one time came to stay with her mother and her mother's lover in the little house in the garden at Mas des Chats. Her mother, Julie, had left home—and had left Emilie there with her father and grandmother—to join her lover, Pierre. Julie and Pierre had lived for a time in the little house.

'I didn't leave home for Pierre,' Julie told me. 'I went because life was impossible for me. My mother-in-law lived with us. She criticised everything I did. My husband's a nice chap—but weak. He's terrified of his mother. I always came second—mother came first. It became unbearable . . .'

Julie wiped a tear.

'And Emilie?'

'I thought she'd be better off with her father—better off staying in the home. She gets on well with her father. She's a Daddy's girl . . .'

But here Julie looked embarrassed.

And after seeing her with her daughter when Emilie came to visit her at the little house, I knew that Julie found it hard to love her child—or, at least, to care for her properly. And Emilie, I could see, may have been a Daddy's girl but she longed to be close to her mother. Emilie, on her weekend visits, was turned out of doors more often than not, to play on her own—or to ride her bicycle, which she did, vigorously, over the grass and flower beds of Mas des Chats in angry revenge.

She also rode up and down the steep and dangerous little bridge leading across the stream to the *colline*. There was a ten-foot drop to the water and no railing. And Emilie, sulky and discontented, wandered alone, her mother oblivious, out into the fields and across them to the farms—a sad little six-year-old in a short white cotton dress.

Emilie's mother was small and so thin she was almost two-dimensional. She was dark, while Emilie was blonde and built on a larger scale than her mother. Julie was permanently anxious, nervous, fragile, her hands trembling, her sleep disturbed. But of the two, it was Emilie who looked the waif.

The cat Emilie reminded me of the child. She also seemed waif-like. She, too, was blonde and larger than her elegant mother Hélène. But Hélène was courageous and determined and Emilie had inherited her mother's characteristics.

'Although I don't think she's very clever,' I said to my sister as we sat by the green swimming pool one lazy summer afternoon. 'I put the food down in one place and she looks for it somewhere else.'

Nora laughed. 'She's clever enough by cat standards. Look what she's been through and survived.'

It was true that Emilie had kept going in all kinds of adversity. When she was about six months old, I had trapped and caught her and taken her to the vet to be sterilised. The day after the operation she had escaped from an upstairs room. She slipped through a very small window and slithered down a sheer wall. She did return to eat—food especially put out for her—but she remained for ever terrified of me approaching her. Once she was very ill. She had become infected, like many of the 'outside cats', with cat 'flu. She sneezed. She coughed. Ulcers developed on her nose and mouth and tongue. A discharge clogged her nostrils. She tried to eat, but the pain of the ulcers must have felt like a burn or the sting of a wasp.

She leapt away from the dish and ran. After a few days, she vanished. I didn't see her for several days. I imagined her dying, hidden away, becoming dehydrated, no longer willing to fight.

Then she turned up, ghostlike again, looking frail and ill. Red blisters covered her mouth and nose. I began a campaign to help her to eat. I put a series of dishes of soft, half-cooked watery fish here and there where I thought she might find them. She did begin to eat, small amounts at a time, and this food perhaps saved her.

It took weeks before she was well again—but she did return to her old strength. She led her life on the fringe of the *mas* in spite of the fierce attacks of Monsieur le Gris and the other cats.

Hélène still acted as mother to both her children, although she was more affectionate to Oedipus.

She could sometimes be seen hunting, a little white cat sitting in a field like a statue, watching for a mouse, then drifting away through the tall grass. She hovered, also, along the rows of cypresses, head raised, ready to leap on an unwary bird—then vanished. Ghostlike Emilie, outcast, loner, not unlike that lonely child wandering through the fields in her short white skirt.

Hélène, Oedipus and Emilie remained closely attached to one another—and their relationship endured over the years. Hélène still acted as mother to both her children, although she was more affectionate to Oedipus. She ran to comfort him when he came in hungry and crying.

His cry was loud and passionate, like the bleat of a lamb rather than a cat. He could be heard calling when he was far away across the fields, running home after a long, exhausting session of mating and fighting, sometimes in freezing weather.

Hélène was troubled by his crying and went to sniff his fur and lick him. Oedipus wasn't always ready to accept her tenderness. If he was very hungry he shook her off so as to concentrate better on eating. But she was the boss. She could reprimand him so sharply he cringed and backed away, although he was much bigger and heavier than she was.

Emilie, on the other hand, longed for her mother's attention. Hélène was often cool towards her, sometimes indifferent. Nevertheless, Emilie felt secure when her mother was around. She came trotting out of her hiding-places in the vineyard and made shrill little cries when the immaculate Hélène stepped out for a haughty stroll. Hélène often ignored Emilie's pleas for attention but I felt that she emanated a stern motherliness, reassuring for her daughter.

Emilie's real friend was her brother. When he was near her, bleating and maaing, she felt confident enough to stand up to Monsieur le Gris and hiss and shout insults at him. Monsieur le Gris didn't dare attack her in those circumstances. He actually trotted away rather nervously, briskly skipping past her.

Sometimes the little clan of Hélène, Oedipus and Emilie behaved in a united, arrogant way towards the other cats, looking as if they were quite prepared to take over the *mas*. This show of strength took place on the terrace or by the swimming pool. They were three fine, strong cats, swaggering. The other cats looked, I thought, a little anxious, but I found their continued attachment to one another moving and enchanting.

32

At Mas des Chats there were a few instances of a kind of nervous breakdown, a crisis of self-confidence, a profound insecurity among the cats.

Katy and Hélène both suffered in this way. The cats, all of them, were in any case extremely sensitive and easily upset. But Katy and Hélène had symptoms, each in her way, indicating a definite emotional illness.

Hélène had always been a melancholy cat with a sad expression on her face. She was easily irritated and gave loud, wild cries when angry or unhappy—which was quite often the case. She seemed at times cynical and bitter and she could be harsh and rejecting with both her children. When she was most distressed I tried to comfort her by stroking her and talking to her, but she was liable to shrug me off and even threaten me with a hissing shriek and bared claws. She was like the least loved child in a human family. I knew she was very jealous but often unable to express her jealousy. I could see her eyes burning from some inner tempest of the emotions if I stroked Baby, for example, while she watched from her position on a radiator on the other side of the room.

Occasionally, she would jump down and come to rub herself against my legs so as to be noticed and have some attention given to her. 'What about me? What about me?' I would quickly try to comfort her.

In the summer she liked to sleep during daylight hours on the bonnet of the car as it stood in the shade of the car port roof. She would come in at night and liked to sleep in my bedroom, provided she was the only cat in the room.

One evening she came hurrying through the cat window looking wild and frightened. I was astonished to see that her coat was drenched—as if she'd fallen in the stream which surrounded the garden. I tried to dry her but she shrugged me off with a warning cry. She turned and ran off again almost at once.

Later, I came across her sitting once more on the bonnet of the car. She was calmer and allowed me to stroke her. But she refused to come

Hélène had always been a melancholy cat, with a sad expression on her face.

Long-limbed Oedipus was a timid but determined ladies' man.

His mother, elegant, aloof Hélène, was prone to strange periods of emotional disturbance.

Hélène's daughter, Emilie, would wait for her meals behind the safety of a lavender bush.

Curly Thomas, veteran of a hundred fights, had the look of an ancient Chinese philosopher.

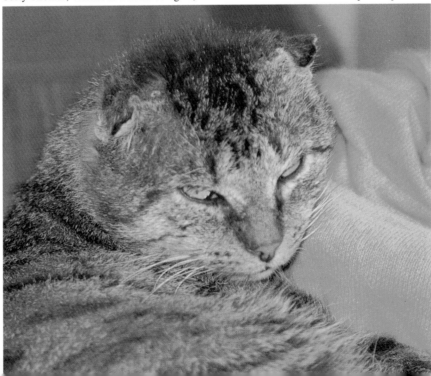

The kitten, Fred Silver, with his *joie de vivre*, brought ripples of excitement to the Mas des Chats.

Glorious Katy, irrepressible vagabond, became Fred Silver's close friend and adviser.

The dog Caramel had become firmly established as a member of the household.

She quickly took to Billy, a sweet and gentle animal who had clearly never known kindness until he found his way to Mas des Chats.

in to the house that night—or even the next day. She remained on the car bonnet. And that is where she lived for the next two or three weeks. If the car was driven out and away, she would lie nearby on the metal lid of the *forage*, the bore-hole with a pump which provided water for the house and garden. As soon as the car returned she leapt up to her usual place on the bonnet.

She began to pretend, and to persuade us to believe, that to set up house on the bonnet of a car was a perfectly normal thing to do. Many people, she implied, do exactly that. And where, she wondered, was her supper? Sheila was staying with John in the little house at the time. She and I behaved like people humouring a lunatic. We agreed that it was quite normal to live on a car bonnet. We found ourselves carrying out her meals on trays, morning and evening. Hélène received her dishes in a dignified manner, making it clear she regarded our bringing food out to her as ordinary practice. She ate enthusiastically. The fresh air gave her a good appetite.

She had obviously had a severe shock of some sort. Perhaps a dog had chased her and she had fallen in the canal. Perhaps she fell through carelessness—but that was unlikely. She was skilful and agile. I suppose she felt safer out of doors where she could escape if necessary. In the house she might have felt she could be trapped.

Whatever the reason, Hélène went on with her *séjour* on the bonnet of the car for at least a fortnight. Luckily the weather was warm and dry. But she was unduly nervous, and on edge. She was startled and anxious at the slightest movement or crackle in the nearby bushes. She had planned, I think, to take refuge, if necessary, in the nearby cypress hedge.

After a while she calmed down. She made brief excursions—to the swimming pool, for example—but she quickly returned to her perch on the car. Finally she decided she felt well enough to go back to the house, after which her behaviour returned to what was normal for her—sultry moods alternating with restrained affection and occasional skittishness.

Katy's nervous breakdown was the result of her being tormented by Monsieur le Gris. But it began with her sliding into a depressed and anxious state. In this mood she was much more timid. As soon as he sensed her vulnerability, le Gris was at his worst with her. The more Katy felt and behaved like a victim, the more aggressive Monsieur le Gris became.

Katy was hounded by him. She became more and more agitated. She didn't know where to go for safety. She climbed onto the mantelpiece and huddled there on a small ledge, like a chamois on a rock in the Alps. She jumped down and crawled into the bottom of a cupboard in the kitchen. Not knowing she was there, I shut her in, accidentally trapping her there for several hours.

Le Gris followed her everywhere, threatening and tormenting. She went upstairs. He went up after her. She came down. He trailed down too.

After a while I knew there was nothing for it but to shut her in a room by herself where he couldn't get at her and she would feel safe. I chose the salon. Katy had spent some time there when she was recovering from the damage done to her leg by a car or motorcycle.

She seemed relieved to be enclosed there. She was exhausted, peering at me with eyes half-closed.

Gradually she revived. Some of her sparkle and energy returned, but she showed not the slightest inclination to leave the room. Instead, she made herself quite at home there. She arranged a little life for herself of a modest, entertaining kind. Being winter, there were several potted plants in the room which, in summer, were placed on the terrace. Sensitive to cold, they had to be brought indoors in winter. There were, among other plants, large ferns with drooping foliage under which Katy hid herself jokily and peered out . . . Tiger, tiger . . . She went from pot to pot, like a general inspecting the troops, snapping sharply at those she felt were slacking. To cheer her up, I gave her a number of toys—five to be exact—three balls of various sizes and textures and two toy mice.

These she gathered into a little heap and then appeared to be counting them with satisfaction. After this she proceeded to subdue them. She attacked one after another, knocked them about, chased the balls around, then gathered them together once more and triumphantly stretched herself across them.

Her favourite toy, in the days that followed, was a small soft ball

Gradually Katy revived. She felt safe shut in a room by herself.

with concentric lines of colour on it. This she happily tossed under every available piece of furniture too low on the ground for her to be able to retrieve it. To Katy's pleasure and amusement, I was forced to crawl about on the tiled floor, fishing out her coloured ball so that she could immediately send it smartly back under.

It seemed to me she felt possessive about the plants and the toys. They were *her* plants and *her* toys, and she was determined to keep them under control—perhaps because the outer world seemed so out of control. It took her several weeks before she felt emotionally strong enough to go out and face that world—and Monsieur le Gris—again. But in the end she was ready to do so. When her confidence returned in full she was a little spitfire, hissing and snarling and letting le Gris know exactly what she thought of him—and very unflattering it was. He was quite taken aback.

33

When Emilie had exiled herself to the vineyard she often appeared with a companion, a very beautiful, bronze-grey male cat with brilliant blue-green eyes. We fed him at the same time as we fed Emilie, two plates being carried out regularly to the vineyard. Sometimes he appeared alone at the sound of a cry summoning Emilie. We called him Patrick in honour of the Brontës.

Emilie and Patrick appeared to be good friends and we were glad she had a companion.

One day Giselle Mabeille telephoned. As usual, she shouted and the line crackled, but I gathered she was asking if I had seen her cat Pinot—and she described Patrick. I replied cautiously, partly because I sometimes wondered if she ill-treated her cats—although I know she loved them—perhaps inadvertently. I said, yes, I thought I'd seen a cat which resembled her description in the vineyard.

She was suspicious of me. I believe she thought I had captured Pinot, was holding him prisoner and not allowing him to return to her. For a while she prowled around the Mas des Chats looking for signs that showed Pinot was with me.

Then one day she telephoned again, elated. Pinot had returned, had had a meal in her kitchen, looked in good health and plump instead of starving. I told her I was delighted—and I was pleased that her anxiety for him was relieved. But Pinot continued to come for meals with Emilie and when, eventually, Emilie decided to come into the house, from time to time Pinot accompanied her. I would find him lying on a cushion in the window of the salon, looking very comfortable and quite at home, while Emilie had taken up her position in a small cupboard nearby.

It was in the winter of my sixth year at Mas des Chats that Emilie suddenly made a determined effort to return to the house and become a part of the inside cat community. Before this happened, she had a period of suffering and anxiety, being chased out of her wits by the dogs, first Caramel, then, more seriously, Billy.

Caramel had been ill for a while. That joyful little dog, normally bouncing with energy and good humour, became tired and lackadaisical. She refused to eat, shivered and lay in the sun, even on a warm day.

We visited the vet. Her abdomen was distended but she had become thinner.

Docteur Arbois suspected her thyroid gland might be underactive, or her suprarenal glands not functioning well. She was to have a test. Blood had to be drawn from her veins at hourly intervals for several hours, and in between the taking of the blood samples, Caramel and I went on little walks. She was not allowed to eat, was hungry and very tired.

By the time the last sample of blood was taken, Caramel was desperate. She let me know I was a savage barbarian. One more needle in her vein and she was leaving home. She never wanted to see a vet again and it was the end of our special relationship. It took me a long time to comfort her. The blood samples were sent off to the veterinary college at Nantes. Nearly three weeks later the results came back—all normal.

Docteur Lamartin saw Caramel next. Knowing her well, he was shocked to see how thin she looked, and said he wouldn't be surprised if she had a cancer somewhere in her body. And her heart-beat was not quite regular. She panted, at intervals, short of breath. An electrocardiogram (Docteur Lamartin's clinic was highly scientific and modern) showed only the slight irregularity of the heart-beat, otherwise no abnormality. Various medicines were prescribed, all of which Caramel adamantly refused to take.

She recovered. Slowly she returned to her cheerful, jolly self. Trotting happily along a narrow, crowded street in Arles, she was stopped by an elderly Englishman in a flowery T-shirt who bent over her crying, 'Oh, what a lovely little doggie!'

With her return to health, Caramel became over-excitable, and with the arrival of Billy, whom she adored, she was exuberant. One day when I came home in the car, she and Billy were waiting for me on the corner of the little road.

Emilie happened to be wandering in the vineyard. Caramel, hysterical with joy, showing off to Billy, lost her head and careered after

With her return to health, Caramel became over-excitable.

Emilie as if she were a rabbit.

Emilie took to her heels and fled. And Billy received a message, loud and clear from Caramel, that Emilie was to be chased. He was still learning from Caramel, not using his own judgement. He chased Emilie for miles and continued to chase her every time he glimpsed her, for months afterwards. It became almost impossible to feed Emilie. As soon as she saw me she flew, believing the diabolical Billy to be close at hand. Billy and Caramel had to be shut indoors, together with Monsieur le Gris.

Then I or Sheila or John, carrying her plate of food, would go out into the vineyard, calling Emilie in a high, falsetto voice. Sometimes she would appear after peering cautiously out from under a tent of vine leaves. Sometimes we had to try again—or try many times. When possible I persuaded Hélène to come with me. If Emilie saw her mother she was more likely to emerge from a hiding place to eat.

One day Caramel, losing her head once more, rushed after Emilie again. I was so angry that Caramel understood, fully, that she must give up this particular sport, forever. She communicated my message to Billy. Miraculously, he too understood and recognised that it had all been a big mistake on Caramel's part. And neither of them chased Emilie again. Even more astonishingly, Emilie also knew that the dogs would no longer chase her. She returned to eat her meals on the terrace or elsewhere near the house.

It was at this point, the beginning of winter, that Emilie decided to come into the house, at least in cold weather or rain. She slipped in, she scampered in, when she hoped no one would notice her. She hid behind chair legs and under tables. She was like a Red Indian, silent, skilful. Her objective was the dining-room where she would lie on the seat of one of the chairs pushed under the table. There le Gris couldn't reach her. The worst he could do—and he did it—was to lie on the table above her chair.

But I persuaded, bullied and coaxed him to give up hunting Emilie. To some extent he acceded to my request.

Emilie became bolder. She crept up the stairs, hid under a bed. In the pouring rain, the icy winds, she was warm and dry—as they all were. All the cats were indoors in the winter weather. At last, the whole cat family was safe, was comfortable. I was delighted. If it hadn't been for the outside cats coming in to eat I might have shut the cat window, closing the city gate, lowering the portcullis.

34

In the summer, water flowed through the canals which encircled the garden and Monsieur Mercier used it for watering grass and flower beds. According to the local custom, at key points the water was dammed by means of boards or metal plates, slotted between two concrete posts, reinforced by sheets of plastic. It could then be channelled wherever needed in large plastic tubes, or simply allowed to run along specially dug trenches.

The customs relating to the flow and use of water went back centuries.

The water was derived from the big canal which ran along the foot of the Alpilles—the Canal des Alpilles. It could be directed at will by the canal authorities in a northerly direction into a network of smaller canals which encircled fields and gardens. The water ran on and on, and allowed miles of land to be irrigated. Those nearest to the main canal had first access to the water. When they had used what they needed, they released the little dam they had created and allowed the water to flow on to the next farmer who in turn dammed and used it, then sent it on.

The water which ran past Mas des Chats flowed on into the Mabeille farm where it was used to water lettuces and tomatoes.

Sometimes, when Monsieur Mercier wanted to use the water, it was cut off a long way away. But one summer the flow was constantly interrupted by an unknown hand, pointlessly it seemed, at a corner of the neighbouring field—one of Giselle Mabeille's abandoned fields. At that corner the canal branched in two directions. By raising or lowering a metal plate the water could be sent either along the field towards Mas des Chats or in an easterly direction along the top of the vineyard towards Madame Corbet's land. If the plate was raised the water ran mainly in the direction of Madame Corbet.

'Did you,' asked Monsieur Mercier severely one morning, 'turn off the water?'

It's not off again, surely? I went to shut the gate only fifteen minutes ago.' He strode across the field to the corner, only to find the metal

The water which ran past Mas des Chats flowed on into the Mabeille farm where it was used to water lettuces and tomatoes.

plate raised once more, mysteriously, by some person, never visible.

'Who can it be? No one else needs water on that bit of the canal. Any ideas?' He shook his head. Water, he told me, could cause a lot of trouble, terrible arguments and quarrels. The water supply was a matter of life and death.

'Men have fought and even killed one another over the water,' Monsieur Mercier solemnly told me, and he patted his spade which might be used as a weapon.

People from the Mabeille farm also came over to see what was happening to their water supply. Two young men, sons of the nearest Mabeille farmer, conferred with me. It was inexplicable, no one could understand it, who could it possibly be, who was interfering with our water supply? They were as puzzled as I was.

I went over to discuss the matter with Madame Corbet. She knew all the local farmers, she knew the people who used water in the neigh- bourhood.

'It keeps happening,' I told her. 'Every time we set the water to flow in our direction someone sends it the other way.'

Madame Corbet couldn't imagine who might be doing this or why. It seemed pointless. She kindly offered to go and talk to Monsieur Moret, the farmer whose land lay on the other side of the canal but who himself drew the water he needed from a point farther up the stream. He was not affected by the cut in the supply.

Madame Corbet let me know the outcome of her enquiry.

'Monsieur Moret says he is not responsible. He says he has nothing to do with it. He has never changed the flow of the water.'

'I can't believe it!' I said despairingly. 'Who else can it be?'

She shrugged. 'There's no reason for him to do it,' she said.

'Perhaps he has a feud with the Mabeilles?' My imagination, spurred by frustration, was taking over from common sense.

'Perhaps,' she said vaguely and smiled—a polite, drifting smile which meant she had done as much about the water supply as she could. As far as she was concerned, there would remain a mystery.

'Could it be her neighbours, the Spanish-Moroccans? Watering their tomatoes?'

'No, no.' That, she thought, was most unlikely. They were far too lazy. The tomato plants were dying, anyway.

The water continued to be diverted. Every time we turned it in our direction, within minutes the stream was sent the other way. Someone, it seemed, nearby, was playing a malignant game, baffling beyond words.

Then, one day, I was walking in the vineyard when, to my astonishment and horror, I saw a sheet of water slowly advancing from the adjacent field, tumbling over the bank and making its way in runnels and ponds between the vines.

The field had flooded. None of us, in our journeys to and fro, had noticed that farther along the canal there were great breeches and holes in the bank (hidden by vegetation and tussocks of grass) which were becoming more and more eroded. The water was pouring in a torrent out of the stream and into the field. Whoever it was who had switched the water in the opposite direction had been trying to tell us what was happening. We had failed to listen.

The canals require careful attention. They must be cleaned every year, the vegetation cut back, the channel inspected, the ditch dug out. Giselle Mabeille's fields and streams had not been cared for, for years. It should have been up to the other members of the Mabeille family to repair the canal. They were the main users of the water and they should have taken on themselves her responsibility. But they were never, in a million years, likely to do the necessary work—partly through idleness, partly because of their quarrels with Giselle.

The only solution was for me to act—to contact Madame Arletti, the *tutrice*, the officially appointed *gardien* of Giselle, who was in charge of her affairs. She must arrange, urgently, before the vines were killed by being submerged in water, for repairs to the canal. I telephoned her at her office in Marseille. 'Madame Arletti,' I said sternly, 'this is an emergency.'

Madame Arletti was an overworked social worker. Giselle was one of fifty people she dealt with in Saint-Rémy alone. I knew from past experience, when we needed to have Giselle's fields cleared because they created a fire hazard, that she would beg me to arrange for the work to be done and she would sanction it.

'I'll try,' I said, 'but you must telephone immediately to authorise him to do the work or send a telegram like last time. You know he won't start without your agreeing.' I was talking about Monsieur Carnot, an obliging young man who owned giant machines which dug ditches, moved earth, harvested corn, cleaned any unwanted vegetation, dug bore-holes.

'Yes, yes!' Madame Arletti promised to get in touch with him at once. But would I let him know what was to be done?

So I found myself (as had happened before) arranging for work to be done in fields that had nothing to do with me—except that their neglect and decay affected Mas des Chats.

Monsieur Carnot, when I could get in touch with him, was obliging. He would do the emergency work immediately, dig out the ditches and block the holes in the banks of the stream so that the vines would not be submerged. But the main job of clearing the streams all around Giselle's property would have to wait until after the harvest.

The ditch was repaired and later properly cleaned in all directions; the vegetation on the banks was tidily removed. All, eventually, was in order. And the unknown hand which had kept cutting the water supply vanished.

The wordless message had been transmitted and received.

35

One shimmering day in early summer, when Nora was paying a visit, we went down to the sea with Caramel. Caramel had never been on a beach. We thought she would enjoy it. We chose the nearest Mediterranean shore, in the Camargue—a vast stretch of sand, untamed and uninhabited, not far from the Rhône's main entrance into the sea. In high summer this is a favourite beach for campers and nudists. Sea birds and flamingoes feed in the shallow inland lakes which lie along the shore. There are dunes as well as an enormous stretch of beach where cars can drive, unless rain has fallen, making the sand soft.

We took a road south, over the Alpilles, turning west and south again. In the Camargue we saw what every tourist expects to see— herds of black bulls and white horses. The skies are huge over the flat land and birds of prey hover high in the air.

To reach the beach, the river Rhône must be crossed by ferry—two or three minutes of enchanting travel.

The Rhône is vast and strong in the last lap of its long journey. The water shines almost silver in the sun and a brisk breeze cools the skin. On board the ferry one might imagine oneself on a cruise, a sea or river voyage, in those moments before it's all over and the car must move onto the land again.

Caramel didn't enjoy crossing the river. Too dangerous, she thought, and she felt safer in the car than on the ferry deck. She was unimpressed by the scenery and hardly glanced at the sparkling hills of white salt—the Salins de Giraud, which are passed before arriving on the shore. And she heartily disliked our walk along the edge of the sea, even though the waves were small and flat. There was too much water, too many pebbles, too much sand and too much space. She let us know, emphatically and pathetically, how she felt.

In the end we were forced to eat our picnic on the edge of the salt lake, the *étang*, looking to the north, the sea and beach behind us.

There the water was very shallow. Sea birds and pink flamingoes paraded and dipped their beaks into the mud below. Caramel endured rather than enjoyed this interlude, refusing lunch.

In the last lap of its long journey the Rhône is vast and strong.

Her most cheerful moment came when we got in the car again to come home. Even then, she made it clear that a long, boring car journey was not her idea of happiness. Next time, if we wanted to do something to please her, an exciting little walk round the narrow streets of a small old town was all she asked.

Nora and I, on the other hand, enjoyed our breath of sea air, the strong, salty sunshine, the flights and landings of groups of pink flamingoes, the gulls' cries and our little picnic on the edge of the *étang*.

36

Baby continued to be addicted to cuddles. She would snuggle down on a chair or on the settee in the salon and squeak two sharp, kittenish cries, demanding caresses.

'Why has it taken you so long, Baby, to come in from the cold?'

The cool, direct stare of her large eyes, shiny as glass, seemed to say: 'Why has it taken you so long to bring me in?' She looked straight into my face, into my eyes, and purred strongly. Her stare did not waver. As long as I tickled and massaged her little body, she gazed at me and purred: 'Ahroom, ahrooom . . .' from shrill to bass, a tiger's purr.

She had changed in other ways. She became very active, darting forward playfully, leaping a little. She chased a ball. I had never seen her do that before. She played with a crust of bread. She twinkled and teased. She looked at me challengingly.

She jumped again on to the chair or settee and rolled on her back, inviting me to yet another cuddle.

While I rubbed her fur, she stretched out four straight paws and braced herself against my arm. She was marvellously toy-like, soft, silky and round, essence of animal innocence. In between times she was her old nervous self, shrinking from me, eluding my touch, running away if approached.

The cuddles were a ritual, to be carried out according to a strict formula—at her request only, in the salon, on a place of her choice. When she chose to be distant in the kitchen, she pretended that she had never met me before.

Meanwhile Katy had another minor crisis of nerves. As usual the cause seemed to be Monsieur le Gris, bullying her and taking over every place she chose to sleep.

The solution, as usual, was to put her in a room of her own at night and keep the door closed. Monsieur le Gris might position himself

Katy had another minor crisis of nerves.

threateningly outside the door or occupy the room during the day (he did both these things) but he couldn't reach her. To be doubly secure, Katy slept under the bed so that even if le Gris managed to break in, he couldn't attack her physically.

Once she was established in her room—which she liked very much—she could be her usual self, quick and light, running, leaping and jumping, bright and brilliant. She herself chose the hour when she wished to be enclosed. She would come into the kitchen and leap up onto the tiled surface where I was busy serving meals to cats and dogs. I might offer her her supper which she would refuse and dash away again. Not many minutes later she would leap up beside me again, and then I knew she was asking to be taken up to her room and have me close the door.

Sometimes she would go upstairs on her own, then come down again to let me know she had gone to her room and would I please come up and close the door? Later I would take her supper to her room. At that point she liked me to sit on the bed so that she could take a flying leap onto my knees.

There followed a tender little scene. Katy let me know how fond she was of me and I did the same for her. After some minutes she was satisfied, jumped down and went to inspect her dish of food. When she was ready for sleep she retired under the bed. And that is where I would find her when I opened the door of her room next morning.

37

Nero must have been fed on *croquettes* when he lived with his two owners down at the farm. If ever he was within earshot, the sound of cat biscuits rattling in their box as they were poured out onto a dish sent him dashing indoors through the cat window. From the way he behaved, I decided that the box had been rattled at meal-times, a kind of gong summoning Nero to his breakfast or his dinner.

When he was very well, he would eat *croquettes* vigorously, crunching them with great pleasure and in large quantities. Becoming less well, becoming ill, he no longer liked *croquettes*—but he still responded to the sound of them rattling in their box. Leaping through the cat window, he would pretend to be interested in the biscuits, push them around a bit in the dish, nibble one or two, and then his eyes would glaze with boredom and apathy. And he was apathetic in general, lazy and quiet. It seemed to me he was gradually failing, although his outward appearance wasn't much changed.

He stayed near to the house—unlike the normal Nero, but a comfort to me. In his weakened state I wanted to keep an eye on him.

He ate, but less than before, and he no longer wanted the drink he used to enjoy, concentrated milk diluted with a little warm water. He lay on the wall beside the guest-rooms which opened onto the terrace, in the shade of a pot of geraniums. He looked tired, although he was still strong enough to leap on the wall in one great bound. And he was more affectionate than ever. The more frail he became, the more gentle and loving he was towards me. In the evening or late at night he would come up to my room to find me. Then, rubbing his fine head against my hand, he would let me know how fond he was of me. He was profoundly calm.

But I became apprehensive and afraid. I knew my cats so well. I saw in Nero a withdrawing of the spirit and I believed he had an instinctive sense of impending death.

One day, as I watched him, he went hurriedly from one resting place to another, investigating baskets, boxes, cupboards . . . I thought, almost without realising what I was thinking, 'He is looking for a place

I saw in Nero a withdrawing of the spirit and I believed he had an instinctive sense of impending death.

to die.' But there was nothing to show me that his death was near, no worsening of his symptoms, no sign that he was in pain.

And then, suddenly, one day it was plain that he was in pain and very ill. At the vet, his temperature was taken. He had a high fever. His kidneys were painful when palpated and a test showed they were hardly functioning. It was thought the infection of his bladder, which he had had for a long time, had given rise to infection of his kidneys.

He was to have an injection of serum every hour or so and a powerful antibiotic. He was distressed and he was in pain—but not, I thought, excessively so. He seemed to be dazed, rather, and also apathetic. When I stroked him, he responded, purred. The treatment worked. He seemed better, passed water and looked comfortable. I shut him in my bedroom, where he went to sleep. And that night, he slept on my bed beside me.

I kept him shut in the bedroom.

The next day I had to go out for a while and left him alone, with the door closed. But the day was warm and I opened wide one of the windows.

When I came back, he had gone. He had pulled the mosquito screen to one side at the open window, and had then climbed down a sheer wall, two stories high, just as Emilie had done.

My heart stopped. A terrible dread came over me, entered my very body as I pictured Nero running away over the hill to die, wretchedly, under a bush as the other black cat had done. I would never be able to find him, never know what had happened to him.

I ran down the stairs—I flew . . .

I tore out onto the terrace—and there, coming round the corner of the house, looking calm and quite unhurt, was Nero. I went quickly to him, scooped him up and took him back to the bedroom. He was unresisting and uncomplaining, his body soft.

Closed in, he didn't object so long as I was there. He had become clinging, dependent on me, wanting me to be beside him. So I stayed with Nero. I left him hardly at all over the next few days, until he died.

At first, the treatment worked. His kidneys went into action again. The vet came to take a blood test, which miraculously showed normal kidney function. But the next day he was ill and in pain once more. I should perhaps have called the vet who had seen him the day before, but poor Nero had had so much investigation and treatment, I thought I would wait twenty-four hours and see how he was in the morning.

I talked to him. I stroked his dark coat. He lay on the bed beside me. He slept at intervals. When he woke he seemed in some pain. Then he slept again, deeply. I thought, 'If only Nero could die (if he must die) peacefully in his sleep.'

In the night, he died.

But not peacefully. He woke from his sleep with a terrible scream— an appalling scream, that went on and on—and his limbs flailed and thrashed . . . until he was dead.

His face was distorted, his eyes open.

How I wished I could have spared him that death.

Shocked, horrified, I sat beside his poor body.

The dawn was about to break. On one of the farms below the hills, a cock crew, a moving cry in the dark, desolate silence. Then another— and another—until the air rang with the crowing of cocks.

And dawn broke.

———————◇———————

Following Nero's death, Monsieur le Gris was in very bad humour, unhappy, angry, grumbling, anxious. Although he and Nero had always been rivals and quarrelled a little, they were also companions and colleagues. He seemed to sense that Nero had died and was greatly upset.

By rights he should have been rejoicing because he was now senior cat, top cat for the first time in his life. But le Gris was an insecure, uncertain cat. The British Army would have called him 'not officer material.' Unlike Nero, he had no ability for authority although he was a bully to the younger cats.

He didn't know how to deal with his juniors, he was up and down in his moods, he was emotionally unreliable.

His disturbance lasted for some weeks. During this time he was particularly unpleasant to Katy, Sugar, Hélène and Oedipus. He was

Following Nero's death Monsieur le Gris was in very bad humour.

impatient also with Baby, who shrank from him as he began to growl at her.

After a while his mood improved, but he never did seem to realise that his dream had come true. He was, at last, in the position of Prime Minister at Mas des Chats.

38

——◇——

For some time after Nero's death, whenever I walked in the vineyard I somehow hoped, magic against reason, to see the dark, dear shape of my black cat lying, as he used to lie, in the shade of the vine leaves, to feel his soft body press against my legs, appearing, as he used to appear, suddenly, out of nowhere. And when, of course, I had to face the reality that Nero would never be seen again, I was overwhelmed by the pain of his loss.

Then, to add to my sadness, Curly Thomas disappeared.

It was in the early spring, when the mating season had begun. Oedipus went off and returned only for hurried meals before rushing away again. Curly Thomas began to make similar excursions, crying over and over again his strange, melancholy cry. He would return, sometimes after only a brief absence, to eat and rest. The weather was cold, sometimes icy. Curly Thomas hurried up to the little basket which stood beside a radiator at the top of the stairs. There, having eaten a large meal, he would recover from the exertion of his trip. One day he went out and came back with another terrible wound on his head. He had obviously been fighting again. I dressed the wound and once more gave him antibiotics.

The wound had hardly healed before he was off again—and returned with a further wound, less severe but nevertheless quite deep.

Then he went out once more—and from this journey he never returned.

Days passed. One day there was a violent storm. Water surged out of the sky and hurled itself on to the land.

I couldn't bear to think of Curly lying perhaps wounded and unable to move under the ferocious beat of that rain. Yet there was nothing I could do, no possible way of finding him. Two weeks, three, four went by. I never saw Curly Thomas again.

There was, I think, a further death—the low-slung, worried old black and white outsider cat who had been coming to eat at Mas des Chats for several years.

He, too, was no longer seen at the cat window. He, too, was missed.

To add to my sadness, Curly Thomas disappeared.

I mourned for all my departed cats, and the spring, hurrying now into the air and earth of Provence, began in sadness.

39

―◇―

Spring in Provence meant cats mating, birdsong, the calling and croaking and singing of frogs awakening from winter sleep, rain alternating with hot sunshine, blossoming almond trees, quickly followed by the flowers of apricot, peach and cherry trees in great orchards.

Spring meant violets and primroses, early tulips, swallows and nightingales swinging out of Africa and drifting northwards, slowly, across the land, red squirrels coming out of hibernation and the unusual maple tree on the edge of the stream producing a great mass of tasselled buds, gold and purple.

And spring meant brilliant light and fabulous sunsets and the sudden arrival of summer.

―――――◇―――――

Summer evening in the town—quiet voices heard through open windows and a snatch of music, a few footsteps echoing on the cobbles. The light of street lamps, discreet and amber, gilds the leaves of the tall plane trees, falls on flowers in window boxes and in pots grouped on window sills and in front of the doors of the houses—petunias, roses, geraniums, pansies—falls on the small leafy squares and secret courtyards and archways and old stones.

An ancient, sweet-voiced, hesitating clock chimes the hours just a minute or two late, followed by another. The new church spire, magnificent in stone, floodlit, towers over the roofs.

The street light falls also on the town cats, gathered here and there, sitting on the bonnets of parked cars, lounging on little walls, on doorsteps and window ledges, strolling in the garden of the museum, communing silently and sliding in and out of lamplight and shadow.

They are well looked after, the cats of Saint-Rémy, both strays and housecats. People put food out for them and most of them look plump and healthy.

The dogs and I pass calmly among them. They are not afraid—and

Spring meant brilliant light and fabulous sunsets and the sudden arrival of summer.

have no reason to be since Caramel and Billy take no notice of them. I look at them all, see there are two unfamiliar black kittens and a marvellous Siamese wearing a collar and bell.

We wander through the narrow streets. Water splashes in fountain after fountain, a cool sound in the warm evening.

40

In the summer the water-lily flowered in the little pond which I had asked Ali, the companion of Marcelle, the *femme de ménage*, to build. The pond was shaped like the segment of an orange, a straight side along the cypress hedge, a curve projecting into the grass around the swimming pool.

The straight side was not quite straight. It should have been parallel to the row of cypresses, but it made a slight angle with them. When I pointed this out to Ali during the pond's construction he would not agree. I was wrong. The line was straight.

Marcelle was called in to adjudicate. She turned her head from one side to the other, then looked at me blandly.

'But it is perfectly straight, Madame.'

She always called me 'Madame' when controversy was in the air. It was clear that she would support Ali whether he was right or wrong. Some time later, long after the pond was built, when we were looking at the water-lily together, she volunteered that the pond was not straight. In addition Ali had failed in the construction of the semicircle. The line wavered. So the pond was a rough and ready shape. Even the thick santolina planted around it couldn't hide its deformity. But the frogs enjoyed it, laid their eggs in it and sang from spring to summer. And the water-lily thrived.

So also did the rushes and irises rooted in pots of earth which stood on the tiled floor of the pond. The tiles could not be seen. Ali, who had perhaps envisaged the clear water of a mosque fountain, had made another mistake. The pond water quickly became opaque. Mud coated the tiles. But the lily thrived. All the summer months, the lily produced flower after flower, exquisite cups of pink and white, floating breathlessly on the still water surface. Lightly they lay, mirrored, pure— lotus, sacred symbol of the East.

After the frogs had laid their eggs in the pond, tadpoles appeared, nibbling delicately at algae and insects at the water surface.

The tadpoles changed slowly into tiny frogs.

Sometimes these minute creatures hopped across the grass and fell

The water-lily thrived, and so did the rushes and irises.

or jumped into the green swimming pool. Some were drowned. They swam round and round the pool with no means of escape.

I placed stones on the top step of the stairs leading down into the water. If they found the stones, they could hop out.

Not all found this solution.

Every now and then I would see one or two floating helplessly on the water surface, gullet bulging, dead.

Tenderly I took their fragile bodies out of the water and sadly laid them by the pond.

41

The deaths of the cats—and the frogs—reminded me yet again of Rosie and her efforts to sabotage my attempts to rescue sad, sick, lost creatures. She objected strenuously to my taking on invalid or what she considered second-rate cats such as Maman and Baby, and she would have maintained that I was doing no good to the group at Mas des Chats by including unfit members. My own nature was such that I felt driven to rescue and restore to health all possible suffering animals, but it was clear to me that Nature would go on as usual, arranging for the species to survive with the strongest and cleverest individuals. The old and the weak and the unwary would perish. Young, strong lives would take their places.

Destructive forces were always going to tug at my cats, who would continue to dance and do somersaults on the edge of the chasm. Some would disappear. Others would arrive to take their place.

And as if to confirm the inevitable rhythms of nature, there appeared, out of the blue, after the deaths of Marie and Nero and Curly Thomas, suddenly, a quite unexpected series of kittens.

There was a knock on the kitchen door, vigorous, urgent. As I went to open it, the knock was repeated with a sense of anxiety.

Two young Americans stood on the threshold—a strong, cheerful pair with fresh and open New World faces. One of them, the girl, held in her hand, to my dismay, a scrap of a kitten, a little bundle of brownish-black fur that gave a small but determined miaow.

The young man also held something in his hands—a carton of milk, a paper cup, a small tin of half-eaten cat food. And a slatted wooden box, which had once transported fruit, also made its appearance. The kitten had been brought with its baggage, its food supplies, its bed, in the hope, presumably, of increasing its chances of being adopted.

They had found the kitten on the pavement outside the entrance to the castle at Tarascon. They were Tourist Tour leaders, taking a group around some of the sights of Provence. The kitten had been sitting on the pavement when they entered the castle with their tourists. It was still sitting in the same place when they emerged an hour or so later. They had looked around for a possible mother cat, and found none.

The pavement around the castle at Tarascon is bleak and empty, stretching to the wall which borders the Rhône. The kitten must have strayed across the road from the busy and bustling inner town.

After much thought and discussion, they decided they must try to save the kitten. They picked up the soft and unresisting little creature and planned to drive it to a nearby area where there were farms and houses with barns and outhouses. They hoped to find a farmer who already had a couple of cats and who might be prepared to accept the kitten.

So they arrived at the crossroads where one road goes up to Les Baux and another to Saint-Rémy-de-Provence. There, they found a young man in a wheelchair sitting in the shelter of an open shed, dozing in the afternoon sun. They explained their mission. He understood. 'There's an Englishwoman who lives near here. She keeps cats. Try her.'

And he described how they could find me.

I listened to this with a sinking of the heart. How many more kittens might find their way to the Mas des Chats on the advice of neighbours?

I was steeling myself to reject the kitten when I thought of Cleo. She was an Englishwoman who lived nearby in a beautiful *mas* with a large walled garden. She had been complaining, when last I had seen her, that the stray cats she used to feed had all disappeared. She liked cats and had always owned some on her farm in England. She might take the kitten.

I went to telephone. There was no answer. Cleo was not at home.

I talked things over with the young Americans, high school graduates taking a year off before going to college. They were working for an agency based in Burgundy, taking tourists around France.

They would pass my way again in a fortnight's time. They promised to return. Meanwhile, I would try to find a home for the kitten. They understood that I already had too many cats. If I wasn't able to have it

They had found the kitten on the pavement outside the castle at Tarascon, bordering the Rhône.

adopted, they would take it to their base in Burgundy where it could be cared for.

They drove away, an energetic, likeable pair. I trusted them.

'They will return,' I told Cleo later. 'If you don't like it, they'll take it away.'

'A likely story!' said Cleo scornfully. 'They were only too glad to dump it. You'll never see them again.'

'They didn't have to rescue it in Tarascon,' I said. 'One can never be sure, but they struck me as reliable and conscientious.'

Cleo very quickly became attached to the kitten. She did, in fact, need some creature to look after at that moment and the kitten was a perfect solution. When the young Americans turned up two weeks later, the kitten had found an excellent and permanent home. They went to visit Cleo, to thank her.

And that was how a lost, stray, dusty kitten from Tarascon—a rather dishevelled, rather poor town of the Midi—came to be a spoiled princess of a cat in Cleo Thomson's elegant *mas*.

Cleo also accepted a second kitten which turned up at the Mas des Chats a few weeks later.

There strolled onto the terrace outside the cat window a very handsome ginger male kitten, about the same age as the female from Tarascon. He announced himself shrilly and complained of hunger. I suggested to Cleo that she should come over and inspect him.

And so two homeless little cats were adopted.

But Cleo refused to take the third.

Some weeks later, the couple then occupying the little house, Sheila and John, heard pitiful cries coming from the vineyard nearby, the cries of a small and hungry kitten. The third kitten had arrived. This time the kitten was black, with a shimmer of paler fur among the dark, giving an impression of silver.

Something in the quality and colour of his fur reminded me of Marie. Was he perhaps one of the kittens she had had immediately before appearing at Mas des Chats?

It turned out he was too old to have been her offspring—but in any case I asked a vet to examine him and take a blood test for *leucose*. Docteur Arbois pronounced him healthy. The test was negative—but

Fred Silver turned out to have indomitable courage, excessive energy and unquenchable *joie de vivre.*

that meant little as he could still be carrying the virus.

When he was old enough, he was vaccinated against this illness—and against enteritis and lethal cat 'flu—but if he had already been carrying the *leucose* virus, he might still develop the disease later in his life.

The kitten was a male, time showed, but in his early days at the *mas* we thought the new arrival was a female and Sheila named it Fifi. Later the name was changed to Fred, and eventually, because of his silvery coat, he became Fred Silver.

I decided, reluctantly, to keep the kitten. Sheila and John very kindly agreed to take care of him during the two months they stayed in the little house. John was particularly fond of him. Fred Silver began his life at Mas des Chats as a cherished and spoiled little creature with two humans doing all they could to make him happy. I feared he might not easily adjust to the more rough and tumble life with the other cats when Sheila and John returned to England and he had to live in the main house.

But Fred Silver turned out to have indomitable courage, excessive energy and unquenchable *joie de vivre*. He threw himself with enormous enthusiasm into the business of tormenting the more sedate cats in residence. They were all horrified—all, that is, except Monsieur le Gris.

Le Gris, a complex character, suddenly revealed a tenderness and motherliness seen before only in his relationships with Baby and Grisette. He behaved admirably with Fred Silver, who hurled himself against the reassuring bulk of le Gris like a wave of the sea at the cliffs of the Dorset coast.

Monsieur le Gris licked the kitten and nibbled his fur, boxed with him, played with him, warned him if he was going too far, and gave him a few brisk lessons in Karate. The kitten leapt on Monsieur le Gris, flew over Monsieur le Gris, assaulted him, somersaulted over him, and gave himself happily to Monsieur le Gris' caresses.

So, with Nero gone, we had a young, joyful creature jolting the older cats into remembering their own youth. Fred Silver, who never stopped purring, brought ripples of excitement to the Mas des Chats.

42

For a few weeks after John and Sheila left for England, Fred Silver was kept indoors in the main house. They hadn't allowed him into the garden unless they were with him. Even then they carried him most of the time. He sat in the crook of John's arm or was tucked in his coat, a little bundle of alert and eager cat.

I was to have the nerve-racking task of introducing him to the outside world. Given freedom, he might race into the fields or over the hill and be lost forever.

Indoors, he flew about like a cat possessed, a small black demon of a cat, bursting and bubbling with violent energy. He chased balls, he chased pieces of bread. He leapt into the pots of the indoor plants, scattering earth. He clawed at them, he chewed their leaves, he climbed up them when feasible.

Then he set himself the task of alarming and disturbing every cat in the place in the hopes of finding at least one who would play. None would. Apart from Monsieur le Gris, they withdrew, like Baby, or shouted at him, like Hélène, or cursed and spat, like Lily. I was forever shutting and later opening the cat window, meanwhile shutting him into various rooms or letting him tear about unrestrained. The sooner he could unleash his energy on the outside world the better for all.

Sheila had made for him a little straitjacket, a wrap-around piece of pretty material with two holes for his front legs and a fastening at the back of his neck. There were two rings at the fastening to which a leash or string could be attached. It was hoped that while wearing this jacket Fred Silver could be guided during his first visits out of doors and learn about the boundaries of the garden.

The jacket was unfortunately not a success. Fred Silver felt uncomfortable when he wore it. He crawled about, his belly almost touching the ground—or simply sat down and refused to move. There was nothing for it but to let him go, holding my breath and crossing my fingers as he tore into the garden and shot off towards the vineyard.

He returned and began to climb trees. He ended up in the maple, a tall tree with many feet of smooth, thick trunk without footholds. To

He set himself the task of alarming and disturbing every cat in the place. Lily was not amused by his provocative prancing.

Fred Silver the descent must have looked like the north face of the Eiger in the Alps, which he was to descend—without ropes or crampons.

He called out to me to help him, pitiful little cries to let me know he was in trouble. There was nothing I could do to help him apart from going to fetch a tall ladder from the garage. The maple stood on the narrow bank of the stream by the little bridge. It would be difficult to place the ladder in position, easy to fall into the stream. I decided in the first place to let him try to make the descent on his own.

I went away to prepare a plate of food to put at the foot of the tree to encourage him to come down. Just as it was ready, Fred Silver scampered in through the cat window. I congratulated him. I could see he felt proud of himself.

That experience dampened his enthusiasm for tree climbing. He didn't go up the maple again but was satisfied with clambering about in the old olive trees on the terrace.

The other cats watched his antics coldly. The only one who looked sympathetic was Katy. Her attitude seemed to imply, 'I was young once and motherless and friendless. I know how it feels. I could teach that youngster a thing or two if only he'd listen.'

At that stage Fred Silver was too busy to listen. He was ecstatic about the marvels of life out of doors—earth, bushes, trees, grass, water, leaves. For days—weeks—he was occupied exploring and discovering.

When he felt he had mastered the geography, the plant and wildlife, he calmed down a little. And then he did begin to accept Katy's advice and superior knowledge. The two became close friends, an odd couple of one-time waifs.

At night Fred Silver was shut in the bedroom next to Katy's, with a little supper. I thought him too small and too inexperienced to dash about in the dark, jumping in and out of the cat window. He would be completely free when he was a little older and bigger. Meanwhile, he slept on the radiator beside the window where he was very comfortable. I let him out at the same time as I opened Katy's door.

Curiously enough, at the same time, another odd friendship came into being. Lily developed a relationship with, of all creatures, Billy

Fred Silver began to accept Katy's advice and superior knowledge, and the two became close friends.

the dog of whom she had once been terrified.

Fred Silver had tried to approach her, dancing and prancing provocatively in front of her, but Lily had responded with a frigid 'We are not amused' and Silver had the sense to leave her alone.

But Billy came and stretched himself out beside her as she lay in the sunlight under the open window. Lily accepted him with calm composure. She looked, in fact, as if she enjoyed the company. I thought I would try to encourage gentle Billy to visit Lily often—a solution to her loneliness.

◇

Once Fred Silver had understood the full potential of the exciting entertainment to be found out of doors, he was no longer interested in chasing balls and pieces of bread up and down the tiled floors of the salon and dining-room in the house. When I offered him the crusty end of a loaf of bread, which earlier he would have been delighted to push around, he rejected it disdainfully.

'When I became a man I put away childish things,' he seemed to say.

The potted plants heaved a sigh of relief. Those not too severely disabled by his attentions began to grow again.

Then Sugar, that Diana of a cat, brought in a mouse which she had caught and killed in the garden. She abandoned it in the dining-room and there Fred Silver found it. He was immensely excited. I could see he was pretending it was still alive.

He had, in fact, convinced himself this was a live mouse and he proceeded to kill it. There followed a long display of ritualised leaping and dancing, of tossing the mouse in the air, catching it, letting it lie for a while, then leaping on it again and tossing it up once more. In the end, he claimed with pride to have killed it, all by himself, just a very small cat and quite a large mouse, his first, and didn't I think he was very clever?

I did. I congratulated him and allowed him to take the mutilated remains to his room when he went to bed.

189

43

—◇—

Oedipus had been away three days. In the night, in my semi-sleep, I thought I heard him call. But when I woke, the cry had been made by a strange cat, wandering on the terrace and calling, as Oedipus so often did, in the hope of finding a mate.

Restlessly I went downstairs, opened the kitchen doors, stood staring out into the moonlit garden, returned to my bed.

I slept, and when I woke again, it was the dawn—or rather, the sunrise. The first pale, dusty shafts of sunlight lay level on the terrace stones and on the grass.

The sky was dappled with a faint drift of mackerel cloud which would melt as the sun rose higher. And as I looked at my quiet garden, I remembered another early morning in Egypt on Gezira, the island in the Nile.

I had gone out for a walk before the heat of the day. Suddenly, I saw through the misty trees the Arab workers coming up from the river, drifting in, slowly, silently, like biblical ghosts, like shadows, in turbans and robes, rimmed in dust and sunlight, moving barefoot in the dry haze. The sun rose higher and the heat struck.

Here in Provence the day was mild, the air clean, clear and light. The sky was blue instead of pallid grey, and birds sang.

I went downstairs again and once more opened the shutters. Just before I stepped out into the fresh morning air, I saw Oedipus, fast asleep. He was slumped on the sofa in the dining-room beside Baby and Monsieur le Gris.

A great wave of relief washed over me. He gave a faint wail and half-stirred. But before feeding him, I went upstairs, light-hearted, to open the doors, first of Katy's room and then Fred Silver's. Katy still slept under the bed and didn't move, but Fred Silver jumped excitedly down from his seat by the window, in brilliant spirits, hurrying to greet me. His purr was like a roll of drums, reverberating.

He stretched himself, happily, from his nose to the tip of his tail. And I could see him thinking, 'Another wonderful day . . .'

He trotted down the stairs and sped across the kitchen floor. I

Off he went in a flying leap, into the sunshine of his first summer.

followed him.

At the cat window he paused, put out his head and sniffed the air. He looked to the left and he looked to the right. Then off he went in a flying leap, into the sunshine, into the warm, embracing air of his first summer.

Then Oedipus jumped from his bed, loudly demanding his breakfast, winding his supple grey body round and round my calves. He was quickly joined by jealous le Gris, competing for my attention. He nearly knocked me over as he tried to oust Oedipus, bumping and butting into my legs, crashing into me with his strong body. Gentle Baby came softly from her bed to be beside him. Then Hélène appeared and went to Oedipus to sniff his fur and comfort him and dapper Sugar tripped in to the kitchen. Katy roused herself from her late sleep, sailed down the stairs, sized up the situation and carried straight on out of the cat window to avoid her enemy, Monsieur le Gris. Lily remained, of course, in her boudoir, calm and dignified but hoping, with a flicker of anxious greed, that I'd soon bring up a tray with her breakfast.

So all the cats of the household had been counted except for Emilie and her I saw, not long after, peering nervously over a lavender bush on the terrace, waiting for her dish, unaware that she was about to be ambushed by buoyant Fred Silver lurking behind another bush.

But she knew very well how to send him packing.

Cheerfully I fed them all—nine cats, nine splendid cats, alive and well and gathered together on this blue and gold morning, this brilliant sun-drenched, summer morning in Provence.